The
Seven Steps
of Agape
Prayer

ROBERT A. WEST

Order this book online at www.trafford.com
or email orders@trafford.com

Most Trafford titles are also available at major online book retailers.

Printed in the United States of America.

ISBN: 978-1-4669-9547-5 (sc)
ISBN: 978-1-4669-9546-8 (hc)
ISBN: 978-1-4669-9548-2 (e)

Library of Congress Control Number: 2013908988

Trafford rev. 05/22/2013

 www.trafford.com

North America & international
toll-free: 1 888 232 4444 (USA & Canada)
phone: 250 383 6864 ♦ fax: 812 355 4082

Contents

Acknowledgments

*M*y special thanks to:

My wife, Louise, for putting up with me throughout the years it took for this book to come into being and for teaching me, through her living, the many ways agape works in the great variety of relationships.

Bill McClure for serving as my muse as he inspired, encouraged, and prodded me from the very beginning of the spiritual exploration that developed into this book, especially during the time when he was the only one reading and making comments about my blog, but most importantly, for showing me the spiritual depth and vastness of the power of agape.

My sister, Carol, for graciously helping me create the family section of this book.

My three sons and grandchildren for inspiring the basis for much of the rest of the family section.

Introduction

*T*he extended prayer practice described in this book came about over a period of several years. Looking back, I realized that during the first few years that led to the practice, I had no idea I would end up writing a book. At first, it was a very personal prayer practice, and I was searching for my own understanding. But writing a book was the farthest thing from my mind.

Prayer and meditation have been an important part of my life. But as this practice developed, I felt like it was something unusual. I was finding a different meaning from all the practices I'd ever heard about. Throughout college, graduate school, and in many ways during the years since then, I'd involved myself in various approaches to praying. At the same time that I was exploring different approaches, I was researching the history of prayer. For inspiration and historical background, I studied references in the Bible. For explorations in the Bible, I found it very helpful to look into the original languages.

One of the areas that opened up for me when I was looking into the original Greek New Testament had to do with a word that seemed to have been misused in the eighteenth, nineteenth, and twentieth centuries during the translations into modern English. When I looked into what was going on with this word, I found that whole sections of Bible study books were devoted to this word because of the problem that there was no English word that could be used to convey the full religious meaning of it. The word was "agape" (pronounced ah-gah'-pay). Long before I realized how important "agape" was to the approach to prayer, I heard the strangest things about that word. I kept seeing the word pop up in all kinds of places, so I started wondering about what the strange word could mean.

Out of all that exploration, I began to make a discovery of something that didn't seem to be covered by anything I'd been exploring about praying. I use the word "praying" to describe this discovery for lack of a better word for it. In the last few years, whenever I showed friends what I was doing, they weren't so sure it fit to what they thought of as praying. But eventually, a couple of other friends encouraged me to put the description of the practice into the form of this book. What I describe here is such a different approach to prayer that I'm not sure a reader would recognize as prayer. But in any case, the full impact of what I'll describe cannot be grasped unless the reader gets involved and tries out what I outline here. Merely reading about the steps of this process will not bring a full understanding of the changes that can come about when the practice is tried over a long period of time. All in all, my motivation for writing is to be helpful. And I found that the writing of this book brought about a deepening of understanding.

When I began looking into what "agape" meant for prayer, I discovered that even though most people who were at all familiar with that Greek word knew it had been translated as "love," yet everyone who tried to interpret the original passages where it appeared admitted that it didn't mean what modern Americans mean by "love." I kept seeing phrases like "divine love" and "the highest form of love." Although even the people who used those phrases admitted that no phrase could capture the full meaning in the way the first Christians, like St. Paul, used it. But I could find very little agreement about the full meaning of what else "agape" can be.

So even though there was a great deal of studied agreement that it has something to do with love, there also was a recognition that there is a theological problem. When I started checking around about this problem, I found that Christians of the first century used the word for *religious* meaning. There needed to be a word that expressed the more profound spiritual sense involved in the highest form of love, but at the same time, the word needed to express a strong motivational connection between religious devotion and action to help people.

So even though several centuries ago, English translations had tried using the word "charity," there were many people who kept testifying that something important was being lost in translation. But I could tell by the way the Jewish followers of Jesus in the first century used it, the spiritual reality behind that strange word played an important part in helping them deal with the many problems they faced in that violent century that became so terrifying for the oppressed Jewish people. Especially during the latter years of the century, when their world was torn apart and the towns of the Holy Land and the temple in Jerusalem were burned to the ground by Roman armies, "agape" gained even stronger spiritual meaning. Underlying everything that they said about what happened in that horrifyingly destructive century was the realization that something had gone completely wrong with human living. As their world was destroyed around them and the first century stretched into the second century, their attempts to live as a community were becoming increasingly more terrifying and potentially overwhelmingly catastrophic, so they began living by the hope that a completely new era of history had to be coming about. And they were convinced that agape, as a spiritual power, would play an important part in bringing in the new era.

As I searched for that original meaning behind what the first Greek-speaking Jewish Christians called "agape," I found myself seeing connections between what I was finding out about that original meaning and our modern problems. So I began to explore how to find ways to bring that original meaning to life in a helpful way for us today. At times, we can feel overwhelmed with our own century's amount of violence and the destruction we hear about as news reports constantly seem to bombard our consciousness. And so this book developed from that search for a way for the meaning of "agape" to help us deal with our problems.

A few years ago, I was struck by a weird occurrence on TV. An international news report about people killing one another in the Middle East was followed by a car commercial telling us that love was what we felt for a car company. Another commercial, for a chain of hamburger places, gave a slogan telling us we loved eating their fast foods, even though those foods were having an increasingly negative impact on people's health. Years ago, I remember a truck that was named after "love," but at least the company changed the spelling to "luv," whatever that is. It has seemed like from the earliest years of my life, I've wondered what was happening to the way people treated one another.

For over a hundred years, modern society has been ruining the meaning of history's most important words. Only two of the many examples are "love" and "charity," which were once linked in the history of Bible translations. Every translation after the King James Version changed the word "charity" in 1 Corinthians 13 to "love." But of course, the word in the original Greek was "agape."

There was an old joke about Sherlock Holmes and Dr. Watson camping out. *They woke in the middle of the night, and Holmes said, "Watson, look up and tell me what you see." Watson said, "I see the beautiful sky filled with the splendor of stars." Holmes asked, "And what does that tell you?" Watson replied, "It tells me that among the vastness of all these stars, we are small and insignificant. What does it tell you, Holmes?" Holmes answered simply, "Watson, you idiot, somebody stole our tent."*

Sometimes, we can miss the most obvious problem facing us because we're not looking in the right way.

For two thousand years, there have been serious people in every generation trying to stop the violence that maims and kills so many people in neighborhoods, cities, nations, regions, and even families. And of course, there have been people trying to find better ways to solve international problems than by resorting to wars. But the twentieth century produced the killing of countless millions of people through violence and cruelty, and the news media broadcasts would lead us to think that there doesn't seem much indication of an end in sight as the human race stumbles through the twenty-first century.

The religious historian Karen Armstrong once said, "Our world is dangerously polarized. There is a worrying imbalance of power and wealth and as a result, a growing rage, malaise, alienation, and humiliation that have erupted in terrorist atrocities that endanger us all. We are engaged in wars that we seem unable either to end or to win . . . . We all face the terrifying possibility of environmental catastrophe." But she also thought, "Yet it is hard to think of a time when the compassionate voice of religion has been so sorely needed . . . . If our religious and ethical traditions fail to address this challenge, they will fail the test of our time."[1]

As I continued searching for the meaning of "agape," I began noticing the various ways the word was being used. "Agape" appeared in the names of churches and ministries, especially youth ministries, choirs, and service centers. But I also heard a comment that because one church called the meals they shared together after worship "agape" meals, some people thought "agape" meant "potluck," just because in one place (in the obscure little Epistle of Jude, verse 12), a meal is mentioned in relation to agape. Over the years since I was in college, I remember reading books that contained a theory about "agape" as one of the Greek words for "love," and I began to notice that theory appearing in all kinds of places, even in sermons given by such diverse preachers as Billy Graham and Martin Luther King.

So of course, I started out trying to get that theory to make sense. At first, I just had a nagging feeling that something was wrong with that theory, but I couldn't put my finger on the problem. Oh, sure, it did seem possible that the Greeks used different words to mean what we think of today as love. That's the only reason that scholars gave for "agape" being translated as "love." But I did wonder why the King James Version (KJV) made such an unusual move as to use the word "charity" to translate "agape" in 1 Corinthians 13 (for example, "Charity suffereth long, and is kind; charity envieth not," whereas the New International Version (NIV) reads, "Love is patient, love is kind, it does not boast, it is not proud").

Over the many years that I served as pastor of churches all the way from urban to suburban to rural, I preached a lot of sermons on what were called the love passages of the Bible. The first several times I preached sermons on parts of 1 Corinthians 13, I remember merely mentioning that "charity" was used in the KJV, but I didn't stop to think what that would mean. And then, when wedding couples asked me to read from that chapter in their wedding ceremonies, I used more recent translations that used our common word "love." Those couples, of course, thought (mistakenly) those verses were talking about romantic love (which the Greeks called eros, not "agape"). Of course, it's such mistaken thinking that has led to the confusion between "eros" and "agape." But eventually, I began to wonder why the KJV translation of those verses gave me so much trouble.

So I started looking into what possibly could have been behind such translation problems. That's when I found out that, actually, what was strange was the Greek word "agape." And the more I looked into what "agape" meant before the first century, the more I began to realize that something was wrong with the way most people today read the New Testament.

Of course, everyone studying the New Testament admitted that the first people to talk about Jesus Christ with Greek-speaking audiences were St. Paul and his followers. So it only made sense that any investigation of the meaning of "agape" had to start with St. Paul. I went back to take a new look at his letters after so many years of preaching about him.

Now, I have to admit that as a full-time pastor all those years, I didn't have much time to spend researching something that didn't seem to make much difference in the lives of the struggling members of the churches I served. Of course, now I'm bothered by that because I wonder why it didn't make much difference to modern Christians—especially since it was so important in the starting of Christianity. Something major did get lost in translation, and that means a whole lot more to the problems of our world than merely an old Greek word.

At least I remembered that everyone I read when preparing those sermons agreed that "agape" was an extremely important word for Paul, and he meant *something far more than love*. So I would mention that Paul did not at all use "agape" to mean what we today mean by our English word "love." But if that's not what Paul meant, then what did he mean? There must have been a reason why Paul, when speaking of spiritual meaning, didn't use any of the commonly used Greek words for "love," (such as "eros" and "philia") but instead chose an uncommon word.

It seemed that people worked hard to stretch the English language when they studied Paul's writings, and they would find it necessary to add extra words to "love." That would produce phrases like "sacrificial love," "moral love," "unconditional love," "spiritual love," and of course, "the highest form of love" and "divine love." But all that still didn't explain *where* Paul got the word "agape" in the first place or why he used a word that no one in many of his audiences had ever heard before and so wouldn't understand.

Why did I start wondering about *where*? Well, that came from many comments I ran into, like the one in the Interpreter's

Bible's notes: "Agape, which was not the common name or usual word for love in those days, particularly so in Corinth . . . . The apostle therefore uses a new word to convey his meaning,"[2] and the comment by Joseph A. Fitzmyer in the Anchor Yale Bible's notes: "Agape was a rare word in the extrabiblical Greek."[3] Fitzmyer guessed that Paul was inspired to use the word because of the Greek translation of Hebrew scriptures—the Septuagint. So "agape" was a rare word and not the common word for love. In those days, nonscholars could only find it in the Septuagint.

It seems like Paul was looking for a different word that specifically wasn't in common usage in the Greek cities where he was helping to start churches. Did he do such a strange thing because none of the usual words seemed to work to express what was almost inexpressible? Was it a case that either they had to find a new word or they had to change the meaning of an old word from the past? It did look like he took the uncommon noun "agape" with its verb forms "agapao" and "agapan" and developed a special role in the spiritual life of the newly forming communities of faith, thus transforming agape's meaning. (Of course, that means that when modern translations use the commonly used word "love," that completely changes what Paul was doing.)

So I tried imagining what it would have been like for Paul as he started preaching to the Greeks of Corinth. In those days, Corinth was a wide-open, fairly wild port city. Because I finally understood that none of the people in Paul's audience would have heard the unusual, rare, arcane word "agape," he would have been met with confused stares. I can imagine there might have been people listening to him who would have said, "What's he talking about? What's this 'agape' he keeps trying to explain?" Only the Jewish synagogues that used the Greek language Septuagint would have even heard the word "agape." Paul probably learned about that from his Jerusalem teacher, Gamaliel. Another place where Paul may have heard about non-Jewish Greeks knowing about "agape" in the Septuagint is among Greeks who had become fascinated with Judaism and so had read Torah in that Greek translation.

So after all these years of looking into what Paul could have possibly been doing in his first letter to those Corinthians, I realized that the part we call chapter 13 was his attempt to explain what he meant by "agape." That's why using the common English word "love" makes those verses even more confusing and, of course, radically alters Paul's purpose. And that must be why the KJV translators purposely did not use "love" but came up with the word "charity" for those verses. But of course, even that word was ruined for use as a translation because of the corruption and change that happened to "charity" starting in the late nineteenth century.

So I decided that not translating "agape" in English versions of the Bible is necessary to understand the religious consequences of what Paul meant. That can be seen when "agape" is left in place of "love" in his conclusion that of "faith, hope, and agape the greatest of these is agape" (1 Cor. 13:13). He was talking about something that was spiritually greater than faith and hope! We need to determine what, spiritually, he could have possibly considered greater than faith and hope.

All this gets a little more understandable when we turn to Paul's letter to the Romans. As Fitzmyer explained, "For Paul the process of love [agape] thus begins in God, whose love [agape] 'has been poured into our hearts through the Holy Spirit that has been given to us' (Rom. 5:5), and this through Christ Jesus."[4] (*"Agape" was added by me because it makes those verses more understandable when we realize that Paul was talking about "agape," not "love."*)

That verse (Romans 5:5) will become more and more important as we move through the following chapters of this book. But for now, just keep in mind that the verse is in the past tense. So when we leave "agape" as untranslated, the whole verse reads, "Hope does not disappoint us, because God's agape has been poured into our hearts through the Holy Spirit that has been given to us" (New Revised Standard Version [NRSV]). Paul was telling them that the followers of Christ have hope we can rely on because God *has already* poured agape into our hearts.

What that passage from Romans meant to me was that for Paul, *agape was a spiritual power* that was there for people, and it could become an active force in the lives of people who made use of it. Then I found the theologian Paul Tillich express the greater spiritual significance of agape by observing that in agape, "ultimate reality manifests itself and transforms life and love."[5] Finally, I began to see that "agape" was the word used to signify the way humans sensed divine manifestation in their lives. To human sensibility, divine Presence manifests to us through agape, so for us, agape is divine action. That seemed to be why Fitzmyer concluded that "agape remains the supreme quality of Christian existence."[6]

The understanding of that last quote shows why "agape" is used when Christians first started translating the teachings of Jesus into Greek for all those people that Paul and his followers had formed into churches. So when the Christians explained the spiritual and moral teachings of Jesus to the Greeks, they didn't use such words as "eros," "philia," and "storge." Paul had convinced Greek-speaking Christians that "agape" (and the verbs "agapao" and "agapan") should be what Jesus would have meant in those important places like "I give you a new commandment: Agapao each other. Just as I have agapan you, so you also must share agape with each other. This is how everyone will know that you are my disciples" (John 13:34-35). (In most places where various linguistic forms of "agape" are meant to appear—and not to be translated into some commonly used word—it was in verb form because for the people of the first century, they were talking about action. The noun form was very unusual, for example, in 1 Corinthians 13 and Romans 5:5. But I'll try not to use the verb forms because for our twenty-first-century sensibilities, we tend to stumble over the verb forms "agapao" and "agapan.")

So now, with that understanding, we are able to see that the Last Supper—teaching section in John is an instruction about the spiritual power of agape. That important point is completely lost to us in the modern world when "agape" gets translated with the common English word "love." No wonder it's so hard today to understand the vast implications of agape as the foundation of Christian identity.

To try understanding what this meant for my personal spiritual well-being, I spent two years focusing my morning prayer time on Romans 5:5. My perspective began to completely change as I was able to sense agape as a spiritual power that God had put into my heart.

Finally, in January 2010, I began a blog (AgapePower.blogspot. com) to try testing out some of the prayer ideas I was exploring. I decided to start the blog because, one morning, while praying about Romans 5:5, I had an intense spirit-filled experience. Although it's a little difficult putting it into words, the best I can do is say that I sensed agape as access. For two days after that original experience, my morning prayer explored what it meant that God had given agape as access. On that second day, I sensed that agape had brought me access to spiritual manifestation of divine presence. Then the next day was when I found this quote from Tillich's book *Love, Power, and Justice*:

> "Agape enters from another dimension into the whole of life and into all qualities of love. One could call agape the depth of love or love in relation to the ground of life. One could say that in agape ultimate reality manifests itself and transforms life and love. Agape is love cutting into love, just as revelation is reason cutting into reason."[7]

What this means to me is, we need such manifestation because the Reality of God is so far beyond the awareness of humans that unless God manifests in some way to us, we have no spiritual awareness. But even at that, we still have to open up to receive that awareness. So then we need some way to access that spiritual manifestation.

This reminds me of Romans 5:2 that talks about having access to God's grace. Such access also can only come *from God*. That's how I now understand Paul's message to the Romans that God gave agape to us through the Holy Spirit. During the last few years, I have slowly been led to realize something very universal about agape: it is the spiritual power that is already deep within every person, as though implanted in us in order to begin our opening process, but it is still up to us to respond in a sense to connect with the power that God has given us for that purpose. I came to realize that agape is not something limited just to Christians. Now I see that agape is something that helps all people everywhere become more truly human. It cannot be limited to any one culture, ethnic group, region of the globe, or religion any more than we can limit the atmosphere of our planet.

So any people anywhere need to let themselves be opened up to the spiritual power of agape and then, through that power, to let themselves sense Presence. In that way, human existence itself is deepened. And then the possibility eventually develops for the whole human race to be helped by letting that openness continue spreading. But agape is not forced on us, so if we don't let ourselves be opened—if we don't let ourselves become fully awake to the presence—agape does not work for us. So unless we accept the gift and are profoundly grateful for receiving it, then it's not of our life.

I used that blog to record the changes in my perspective about the spiritual meaning of agape. And of course, I experienced changes in my understanding of prayer. As months went by, I began to learn a different way to pray. I learned that prayer could be a way of opening up to the power of agape. But also my awareness was expanded to sense agape influencing the relationships of my life. It was as though agape began flowing up from my spiritual depths and began flowing out from me during other parts of my day as I related to people around me. Then when I returned to take that new awareness of all that into my prayer time, I began to think about a different kind of flowing in prayer—I began to pray for agape to be sent out to people I was concerned about. Eventually, I explored both the effect of agape on my life, and also I speculated about what all this meant for solving the problems of the modern world.

In one blog posting that was on Martin Luther King's birthday, I decided to devote that posting to his memory because he truly understood the power of agape. He let it draw him into actively confronting all those people who considered him their enemy. He said,

"When Jesus bids us to love our enemies, he is speaking neither of *eros* nor *philia*; he is speaking of *agape*, understanding and creative, redemptive goodwill for all . . . Only by following this way and responding with this type of love are we able to be children of our Father who is in heaven . . . . Agape is the love of God operating in the human heart."[8]

He knew from hard experience what agape power could do when it worked in a person's life and in a group, a nation, and the world. Rev. King saw firsthand how agape power poured through the Holy Spirit into people to give them courage and strength to endure all things and to work to overcome the terrible oppression against them. He talked about agape as creative, redemptive power, and he said that by following this way of agape are we able to act as God intended humans to act. He deeply believed in and put into action, as he mobilized masses of suffering people, the power of agape. Through those years of the civil rights movement, the evidence became clear that agape was the most lasting way to truly change the way people lived and then be able to change social conditions. Rev. King had seen also the horrendous evidence that the alternative was the impossible situation in which "returning hate for hate multiplies hate, adding deeper darkness to a night already devoid of stars."[9]

Looking back on those days, we can see that a turning point in history was happening around them. I can't help but think that such a change was also a demonstration of a part of the power of agape. Of course, there also had to be the marshaling of many other methods, including the changing of laws. But using worship, prayers, and songs had shown Rev. King how spiritual power could help large numbers of people to gain the justice they were being denied under a corrupt system of laws, and so the basis he relied upon was the agape power of nonviolence.

*   *   *

So, slowly, I was led to the conclusion that Paul would not have wanted "agape" translated as "love." Finally, I decided to get a better grasp of how the New Testament would have read if Paul's understanding had been followed. So I took the important passages that originally included "agape" and left the word untranslated when the other words are translated into English, then I printed out those passages. Reading through all those verses had such a profound impact on my understanding of the meaning of agape that I then posted those verses as a block of text in my blog on August 20, 2011. That list of selected New Testament verses appears in the appendix of this book.

Each chapter of this book of agape prayer involves an expanding cycle of prayers. The first step is about a method of allowing ourselves to be opened up. But it is also about waking up to find agape as a gift for you. Once you have relaxed completely into a profound realization of agape spreading from deep within your heart-center, permeating your being, bringing into your imagination a sense of what it would be like to fulfill your well-being and deep joy, then you are ready to move on to the next step by praying for other people.

Chapter 2 describes holding in prayer a deep desire for agape to flow in the life of a close, respected person. During each of the following chapters, the rest of the steps describe an expanding list of people to pray for: a dearly beloved friend or family member, then a stranger, then someone who may be hostile to you (even an enemy). When the soft, warm, comforting feeling of agape has formed in you about those people, then expand out to a group of people, then out to communities, nations, continents, and finally, all of Creation. This can be accomplished because of the realization that the spiritual power of agape brings us a way to connect with others while connecting with divine presence. In the last chapter, we will come to the broad perspective that allows us to see that one of the main purposes of the agape prayer is to facilitate the flow of agape among all people.

When you are ready, turn the page.

Notes

1. Karen Armstrong, *Twelve Steps to a Compassionate Life* (New York and Toronto: Alfred A. Knopf, 2006), Borzoi Book, 5.
2. *The Interpreter's Bible* (New York and Nashville: Abingdon Press, 1953), vol. 10, 166.
3. Joseph A. Fitzmyer, *The Anchor Yale Bible: First Corinthians, vol. 32* (New Haven and London: Yale University Press, 2008), 489.
4. Ibid., 490.
5. Paul Tillich, *Love, Justice, and Power* (New York: Oxford University Press, 1954), Galaxy Press, 33.
6. Fitzmyer, 490.
7. Tillich, 33.
8. Martin Luther King, *Strength to Love* (New York: Harper and Row, 1964), Pocket Book Edition, 44.
9. Ibid., 44.

CHAPTER ONE

Opening Up to Agape

When a lot of people think about praying, what often comes to mind is the kind of praying that is asking for something, either for themselves or for others. That's not what I'm talking about. This book is about a different kind of praying.

We can start taking the first step by using a kind of praying that can be thought of as opening up and finding. Then this way of praying leads to six other steps, and I devote a chapter for each step. Chapters 2 through 4 are about holding others in prayer as individuals. The final three chapters expand the prayer practice to groups, then out in the ever-widening circles, and finally, beyond people.

When I say "opening up and finding," it's more like what is described in Psalm 62:5-8, "Truly my heart waits silently for God; my hope of deliverance comes from God . . . . Trust always in God, my people, pour out your hearts before God" (the New English Bible

[NEB]). If we think of "finding" as being illustrated by taking a spiritual perspective of the kingdom parables of Jesus, we are looking for what is at the true heart of life. And when we take that into the spiritual aspect of relationships, we are seeking what is truly best for the *ultimate* well-being of people. So gaining insight into our own spiritual well-being is merely the beginning. To find what is one's own ultimate well-being, we are led to a relationship— to opening up to others and finding what ultimate well-being is common to all people everywhere.

As I explained in the introduction, my prayer practice led me to the living meaning of Romans 5:5. The hope expressed in that verse and in the parables of Jesus is not in vain. That realization only came into full understanding for me, of course, when I finally concluded that all English translations had changed the meaning of that verse. Finally, I tried reading it by leaving the Greek word "agape" untranslated. As I described in detail in the introduction, a profound shift in perspective happened when I realized that Romans 5:5 was proclaiming something of ultimate meaning with the words, "Hope does not disappoint us because God's agape has been poured into our hearts through the Holy Spirit that has been given to us."

As I began to put into practice the deeply spiritual meaning of that verse, I began to sense it as divine blessing. The gift of agape is a divine blessing. And as people use agape in the way it was intended to be used, we take part in the expansion of that blessing. So when we share agape with those around us, we are sharing divine blessing with them. It is that shift in perspective—to consider agape to be a spiritual power conveying divine blessing—that led me to this prayer practice explained in this book.

*   *   *

It may seem obvious to say that a person needs to be ready for this prayer practice in order for it to mean anything, but that's what happens. I can remember many times when I've run across old books that I'd read years before, and yet as I reread them, they meant a lot more to me. Sometimes I find a deeper helpfulness in the book that I didn't receive the first time I read it, and I realize that happens because I just plain wasn't ready to be helped the first time I read it.

So this first step needs to begin with getting ready to receive. We need to develop a prayer attitude of being "silently" open so that we can be awakened to a spiritual power present in our heart. But it's not a prayer that asks for something to happen; instead, it's much more profound than that.

It's not even about asking for a spiritual power called agape. When Paul gave Romans 5:5 in the *past* tense, he was saying that we don't have to ask for it. The gift is already there in your heart-center. So this type of prayer begins as a method for waking up to what is deep within.

My research about agape in the writings of Paul and in the Gospels led me to see how that insight about agape from centuries ago can have a profound impact on a person's prayer life today. When I finally woke up to that impact, it became a present reality in a way that I sensed agape coming up from deep within. For me, it slowly brought me a sensation like that of spiritual energy flowing from my heart then permeating my whole being. And so that sensation of spiritual flowing took on deeper meaning as I've slowly learned that this spiritual awareness has an impact on my relationships. That impact began to happen as I sensed agape coming to life around me. What I've been able to conclude is this: people already have the divine power of human relations active deep with their heart-centers. And it needs to be released into the work of their lives.

The professional work of my life was as a pastor. When I think back over the years of working with churches, there are a vast number of memories of relationships. I learned much about the impact that agape had both on my personal faith development and on deepening relationships. And the learning is still going on in such a way that I know I have a lot more to learn.

One of those many examples was of the day when only agape sustained me. This happened at a period of development when I was just beginning an awareness of the meaning of agape. The day had started with beautiful spring weather, but I was having a little trouble appreciating the beauty because I was nervous about an end-of-the-day pastoral appointment I'd made with a disgruntled member of the church.

So I went for a walk to clear my head. The May weather in Colorado was spectacular, and as I took in the aromas of flowers and viewed the newly green trees, my mind emptied of all concerns. But after a while, I began to get an intuition that I needed to go to the church office. By the time I got there, the part-time secretary of our little church had left for the day. As soon as I arrived at my desk, the phone rang. On the other end of the line was the upset grown daughter of a longtime member, Irene. Over the years, I had become especially close to Irene's family. Before her health gave out, she had been a devoted choir member and deaconess for many years. A couple of years before that day, I had conducted the funeral for her husband and had helped her in her grieving. The phone call came because Irene had just suffered a terrible heart attack but was refusing to go to the hospital. Her daughter was convinced Irene was close to dying. The daughter was calling for my help to convince her mother to go to the hospital.

I hurried to her home, and the worried daughter met me at the door then led me to the bedroom, where Irene was in bed, barely conscious. As we sat on straight-backed chairs on either side of the bed, I could tell that it was too late for any hospital to help. With her daughter crying beside her, all I was able to do was to hold Irene's hand and pray with her as her life slipped away. The window shades had been closed, but there was still enough light to see a table with a display of family photos. When I glanced over the photos of her deceased husband surrounded by photos of their children and grandchildren, I was filled with memories of the family gatherings in the church and of all the work Irene and her husband had done in the church. I felt agape flowing between us, bringing peace and strength for facing what was happening. While we prayed with her, she died. Her daughter became very distraught, and it took me several minutes to calm her down enough to start phoning other family members.

After a few hours, following the arrival of two family members who helped make the proper arrangements, and after I had prayed with the family, it was time for me to leave for that appointment I had been dreading. At that point, I was emotionally drained, and I should have just canceled the appointment, but as I slowly found enough energy to get out to my car, I sat for a few minutes and renewed my awareness of the agape that had been shared in that moment of dying. As I prayed, I was filled me with the confidence that agape would sustain me. So I drove to the home of the disgruntled member.

His grown daughter answered the door and had an apologetic expression on her face. We walked through the house to find her father in the kitchen. On the way to the kitchen, I realized that all I could rely on in that moment was God's agape, and so as I walked, I opened myself to sense the flow of agape. The daughter brought us coffee and cookies. As I slowly munched a cookie and sipped coffee, he began his harangue that displayed his prejudice against lesbians and gays. It quickly became obvious that he had a major problem with his homophobia. He had just learned that the denomination of our church was the first denomination in which lesbians and gays could be openly ordained as clergy. The man's daughter disagreed with him and was obviously embarrassed by his attitude. I had to focus deeply on agape to keep calm and not let his hateful harangue overcome me. I had no energy of my own left and had to completely rely on God's agape. Whenever I tried answering him with rational arguments, I could tell that such a response had no effect because he was not in a reasonable mood. Through the power of agape, I was able to see that all I could do was let his words float off into the air. After he was finished, I swallowed deeply, thanked him for sharing his concerns, thanked his daughter for the coffee and cookies, and walked out of his house. I had not accomplished anything except to listen to his complaint. Eventually, he left the church.

Somehow I made my way out to the car and drove home to the comfort of my wife and children. As I looked back on what had taken place in that kitchen, I realized that for about an hour, all that sustained me was the energy of agape.

During those intervening years since that day, I gained many new insights and underwent strong spiritual growth as I let agape work within me and throughout my life. Now, as I said before, I know I still have a lot more to learn.

*   *   *

Over a period of several years, as I combined my daily meditations and experiences with searching through Paul's writings, I experienced a growth in the meaning for the word "agape." I was led deeper into that search because I kept having the feeling that I was missing something. But what kept me going in searching came when I started finding, through prayer but also through deepening relationships, that the word "agape" could be used to describe what was almost indescribable in life.

As I explained in the introduction, I began my years of searching by looking into the translation problems. The increasing use of "agape" in the first century began in a similar way as the word began to find renewed use in the nineteenth century: people began to realize "agape" as a *spiritual* term. It was not used in common Greek language as a word for "love," but appeared almost exclusively in religious writings.

This religious practice was the basis for using "agape" by the seventy translators of Hebrew scriptures into Greek (called the Septuagint). And that became the basis, when translating the teachings of Jesus into Greek, to use "agape" in places like the two great commandments. Later, when those Greek religious writings were translated into Latin, "agape" was translated as "caritas" (probably pronounced "chār'itis")—which the Latin churches made sure had a spiritual meaning (because it was not the Latin word for "love"). Six hundred years ago, when those religious writings were translated from Latin into English, it was transliterated, using an earlier French translation from "caritas" to "charity." And I guess that might be why "charity" eventually started to be used for the religiously motivated acts of helping people by doing works of feeding, sheltering, clothing, educating, counseling, comforting, forgiving, and providing the necessities of drink and medicine. Their reading of the New Testament led them to see these understandings of charity as acts of justice-making. The divinely inspired goal was to help oppressed people rise out of poverty. (But maybe that was why many people in authority positions began degrading the word "charity" until today; it has lost all its original spiritually inspired justice-making meaning. Especially, many political authorities were afraid of the changes the original meaning was bringing about in society.)

But as I came to realize that there was no English word that expressed the whole scope, from spiritual to compassionate to justice-making meaning, that Paul had put into "agape," I decided to try studying the New Testament with "agape" left as it was meant to be. So when I began rereading the Gospels by leaving "agape" in place, not translated, I came to deeper understanding of what Jesus was trying to show when he added a second great commandment. So it's possible to understand Matthew 22:37-40 this way:

> *"'You shall share in the agape of the Lord your*
> *God wholeheartedly, and soulfully, and mindfully.'*
> *This is the first and greatest commandment. And a*
> *second is like it. 'You shall share God's agape with*

your neighbor as you yourself [share in it].' On these
two commandments hang all the sacred way."

(From now on in these pages, when I use biblical quotes, I will follow that practice of doing as I believe Paul would have wanted and leave "agape" in its original Greek, but because we tend to stumble over the verb form of agape, I'll change "agapao" and "agapan" to expressions like "share agape with" or "show agape for" or "share in agape," for example, "Knowledge makes people arrogant, but agape builds people up. If anyone thinks they know something, they don't yet know as much as they should know. But if someone [*shares in the agape of*] God, then they are known by God" [1 Cor. 8:1b-3, the Common English Bible (CEB)]).

So when we read Jesus saying of the great commandments "A second is like it," we see that what is in the second commandment that is "like" the first is agape. And the spiritual power of agape becomes the way the first great commandment leads us to see, as a religious commandment, the need to care for other people.

So an additional insight opened for me as I worked with agape in the relationships of my life. Slowly, I began to realize what it means for agape to be already in other people's hearts. As we hold other people in prayer, we can be aware that they have agape within themselves. And one way for a lot of people to know they need to wake up happens when they see they are missing something when they deny that this special spiritual energy is already inside them.

In Luke, the profound awareness that agape links together the two great commandments is followed by the parable of the good Samaritan. So that parable becomes an illustration of how agape works in human relationships (thus overcoming all artificial, cultural barriers and divisions between groups of people, such as the Judaeans and Samaritans). That awareness is the basis for the other steps in this prayer process that are explained in the chapters following this one. And as the parable shows, agape brings the spiritual empowerment to people to actively help others. And so finding the deeper meaning of that parable is helped by remembering how Jesus shocked his Jewish listeners by using a Samaritan in that parable in order to break down barriers of prejudice between groups of people, even groups who historically hate one another, as the Judaeans and Samaritans did at the time Jesus told the parable. I think he used the characters in that parable to teach a lesson for all generations: that we should let agape help us stop the practice of blindly continuing prejudices and persecutions against people who are different and thus not understood.

*   *   *

The lengthy prayer practice begins by preparing your heart, your soul, and your mind to be fully opened to recognize agape in your life. So you pray to wake up to the presence of a gift for you from God. My search for what Paul meant by agape produced the awareness that agape is the spiritual gift that is meant to wake up a person to divine presence.

The seven steps of this practice follow the pattern that can be discerned from the gospels, in which Jesus called people to him so he could show agape in action, and then he would send them out to function as agents of agape. So the first step is to become aware of agape. That's what I meant by "finding." Each of us finds in his or her own way the spiritual power of God's agape. So it's important to know what has been found or, in some people's case, what has found them. A person needs to experience receiving in order to know what to pray to send. So this first chapter is about the spiritual experience of waking up, opening up, and finding.

Agape begins the opening process, but it is still up to us to respond in order for the opening up to divine presence to continue. But agape is not forced on us, so for those people who don't let themselves be opened—who don't let themselves become fully awake to the Presence—agape does not work for them. But for those people who do awaken to the power of spiritual agape, they grow in understanding about living through the spiritual energy.

When we're trying to find the way agape is a gift, it might be helpful to imagine Christmas morning as a child. Look deep within yourself to find the moment of joy-filled excitement over receiving a wonderful gift. Now, from a sense of deep prayer, seek to find agape with the same kind of joyful excitement that you find a gift you have been wanting to receive.

Let yourself feel the spiritual joy as you begin finding a vision of your well-being. Let a picture develop in your imagination of what would fulfill your life. Try to sense what that would feel like as your living is affected. Then sense how the spiritual power of agape is the basis of that. You may have the spiritual sensation of that as very much like intimacy, but it is a spiritual intimacy. Let the spiritual sensation come to you so you experience being drawn close to and opening up both to Presence intimately and to the vastness of eternity.

*   *   *

As I said in the introduction, my own preparation for finding this prayer practice began by spending two years in early morning prayer that began by focusing my praying on Romans 5:5. I needed to practice becoming fully aware of what agape feels like as it opened me up spiritually. Then one morning, I was sitting outside, and I started thinking of a few people in my life that I was concerned about. At first, I didn't realize what was happening. Then slowly it came to me that I was prayerfully participating in a spiritual process that felt like I was sending agape to them. Of course, the normal concepts of space and time had no bearing on what was happening because prayer is not limited by such humanly constructed concepts. From that point on, I started a practice of repeating that process every morning. And seven steps expanded from that practice as I prayed for an expanding list of persons (a few of the steps took a long time to develop, so I didn't move from step to step until I was fully ready).

Of course, these steps are only possible for us because agape is not being generated by us but is actually the way the divine presence is made manifest to all that God creates. Obviously, this prayer practice should lead to action—to the power of agape actually flowing through your life's work, out to actively helping the lives of people and to the care for Creation.

As my awareness of the power of agape grew, I found that my perspective on life was changing. For example, it became important to realize that agape doesn't cause us to be more anxious, but it brings us a way to ease out of being anxious. So it doesn't force us to become something; instead, it helps bring us closer to a deep sense of what is important in life. One way it helps us is with a deeply calm strength to *be* what we were created to be. That was one way that the agape understanding of 1 Corinthians 13 helped me come to a new awareness of the meaning of Matthew 5:48, which used to be translated as "Be perfect, therefore, as your heavenly Father is perfect" (NIV). Of course, that verse, when taken out of context, has caused a lot of misunderstanding and a lot of problems over the centuries with people trying to be perfectionists. So the latest translation of the Bible (when I leave "agape" untranslated) has that verse read, "Therefore, just as your heavenly Father is complete in showing agape to everyone, so also you must be complete" (CEB). The Greek word that was translated as "perfect" meant "that which is at the end." As it was used in the Septuagint, it meant "sincere," "honest," "upright." In Ephesians 4:13, it referred to someone who is mature. So the Common English Bible translated it as "complete." Now, what does agape show us about the true meaning of that verse and its full context?

In the first place, because this is part of a section in both Matthew and Luke that deal with agape, I was able to see that the Lucan verses are better expressions of agape. "Be merciful, just as your Father is merciful" (Luke 6:36, NIV). (Or as the CEB translated it, "Be compassionate just as your Father is compassionate.") In a sense, when a person truly, profoundly opens up and realizes the agape in her or his heart, there develops an awareness of what it is to be what people were created to be. But at the same time, we see that awareness as different from some humanly fabricated ideal, so we don't need to get all worked up and frustrated trying to act according to some ideal we're not. As Paul said, "Agape is patient and kind" (1 Cor. 13:4).

So it looks like in the teachings of Jesus about agape, he was trying to point out that it wasn't something for us to intellectually understand because the reality went so much more profoundly deeper than mere intellect. And it wasn't something we have to make ourselves believe because there is no point in making ourselves do or become something we already are. It was more a case of being (*be* complete in showing agape to everyone," with the emphasis on "be" as in "you should just *be*")—a case of finding agape already in us and then letting it be in us in a way that allows us to relax and live fully as we are created to live.

That's the way Luke's version shows us how God is merciful and compassionate and so we can be, first, merciful with ourselves, and then merciful with others. Or to use the words of Paul in 1 Corinthians 13:4, let agape help you start by being patient and kind with yourself. There is a sense conveyed in those verses of just being natural—that such is what life is all about. And there are a lot of people in our modern world who desperately need to be merciful, patient, and kind with themselves. This can become true especially for you when you realize, deeply, that you can forgive yourself. Agape gives you the basis to do that when you completely open to it.

That seemed to be why we find a transition between what we call 1 Corinthians 12 and 13. In chapter 12, Paul appealed to the church to let people develop in their own way whatever their talent is. But then he went on to show that an even better way in a faith community is to let agape be the power to help people *be* what they were meant to be and to help people relate to one another. So chapter 13 starts with a list of what people were prizing as spiritual gifts to make themselves feel more important than other people, but after each of those gifts, Paul showed that God's gift of agape to every person was actually the ultimate spiritual gift.

The understanding there is that agape is the way God gives meaning to the human search for the wonders in life. Agape is God's way of opening us up to all that is wondrous. Paul put it in these words:

> "If I speak in tongues of human beings and of angels, but I don't have agape, I'm a clanging gong or a clashing cymbal. If I have the gift of prophecy and I know all the mysteries and everything else, and if I have such complete faith that I can move mountains, but I don't have agape, I'm nothing. If I give away everything I have and hand over my own body to feel good about what I've done, but I don't have agape, I receive no benefit whatsoever" (1 Cor. 13:1-3, CEB).

When Paul said "If . . . I don't have agape, I'm nothing," was he saying that we are nothing without agape? Did he mean agape is of the very essence of life—that it brings such fullness to existence that we can't find ultimate meaning in existence without it? That seems to be his point when he got to the climax of this section and said that the effectiveness of all the other spiritual gifts will eventually end, but agape will never end. Agape in our heart-center is what is eternal. And we constantly keep in mind what Paul meant in Romans 5:5 that he deeply believed we already have agape poured into our hearts. So what's implied in the conclusion is that each of us needs to connect with the agape that is deep within us—at the very heart of our being—and let it work in our life in order to become fully mature in our spiritual development.

Then Paul threw light on the negative so as to mean that if we don't realize the full power of the agape that has been poured into the heart-center of every person, we remain childishly unaware of the spiritual dimension of life (13:8-11). To expand on this, we also remain unaware of the great possibilities that are there for us to live.

After describing how utterly important agape was to living fully as people were meant to live, Paul began his detailed description in verse 4 of what agape brings to a person's life. Now, some of his first readers might have been surprised that he began with patience. (And I imagine that most impatient Americans are also surprised that patience is at the very heart of agape.) But again, he was speaking spiritually, so I think he was starting like that in order to say that agape shows us a way for God to be patient with us. And it's a good thing that patience is at the heart of agape because there are a lot of starts and stops and restarts that come with the agape prayer practice. So patience is utterly necessary, not only for our spiritual development, but also for our existence. So that's where we begin.

That's the way it happened for me, anyway. It took a long time for me to realize that agape was not just there for me in my morning prayer time but was there for me during all my busy daily schedule. Of course, I have to remember to open up to agape when I'm the busiest. Agape is meant to be a helper for us in many ways throughout our lives. And so agape doesn't go away when we ignore it. It functions as a presence that patiently waits for us to use. That's why Paul added a second part of verse 4: "Agape is kind." It doesn't get locked up when we feel guilty because we forgot during some hectic time to pause long enough for agape to flow through us. And I have to admit that there still are many times when I forget to look within to find agape to use in relating with other people. So when we stop feeling guilty (or feeling sorry for ourselves), then we can merely relax a little and let agape open us up to what is ultimately important in that moment. In other words, agape can bring us fully into the present moment, when we let it.

The implication behind all this is that we are to learn from agape working in our life. And that means learning in the deep, spiritual, transformative way. So as agape influences our deep understanding of life and then influences our way of relating to others, we are slowly transformed. We find a new perspective on what works best in relationships.

Because Paul began with patience, he implies that patience begins our learning about what agape brings throughout our living. The King James Version uses the expression "suffereth long" instead of "patient." That adds a new depth of meaning for all those people who wrongly want religion to guard them against suffering—to somehow keep pain and tragedy from happening to them or to their loved ones. Of course, we don't want our loved ones to suffer. But we get nowhere by pretending that it won't happen. So we need to face and be honest about the painfulness and tragedies of life. What everyone needs is a way to creatively handle and learn from whatever comes our way in this often crazy (and yet amazing) adventure of living.

So we are meant to find that agape is the spiritual power that helps everywhere, teaching us throughout every aspect of living, even in suffering—especially in suffering. But it is never meant to stop pain and tragedies from happening to us. Maybe that's the hardest lesson of all to learn, but learn it we must. And also maybe that's why patience comes first in the list. If we don't learn patience, then everything else in life becomes harder. Patience develops for us in life as we slowly realize that agape works to bring us into divine presence in every moment. That's why Paul said that agape "puts up with all things, trusts in all things, hopes for all things, endures all things" (verse 7, CEB). I think that Paul knew firsthand that people can't escape from tragic things happening to them, and so there is no point to trying to pray our way out of having to experience pain. Instead, we find in agape a spiritual power to help us get through the pain and heartache, and then we can transform tragedy into creative energy that can help us. So the transforming power of agape is not for what is outside us but is for what's inside us. But it is then up to us to use what we have learned through agape for the advancement of the common good, and eventually, we can do whatever comes our way to do for the betterment of all people.

In those verses that follow the statement of agape as patient and kind, Paul seems to be implying that agape is our very witness that true spiritual power is on the side of patience, kindness, justice, and truth, and that it is against envy, conceit, self-righteousness, and any desire to act judgmentally. There is a conclusion involved in those verses about what happens without the inspiration of agape. Negative behavior comes about when agape is ignored.

Paul approached from a little different angle in Galatians when he said, "You are called to freedom, brothers and sisters; only don't let this freedom be an opportunity to indulge your selfish impulses, but serve each other through agape. All the Law has been fulfilled in a single statement: show agape to your neighbor as yourself" (Gal. 5:13-14, CEB). He concluded by saying, "If we live by the Spirit, let's follow the Spirit. Let's not become arrogant, make each other angry, or be jealous of each other" (Gal. 5:25-26, CEB). Several verses later, we are advised that spiritual guidance is against selfishness. The image of harvesting what we plant is used: "Those who plant only for their own benefit will harvest devastation from their selfishness, but those who plant for the benefit of the Spirit will harvest eternal life from the Spirit" (Gal. 6:8, CEB).

We can express that in modern language by talking about how we view identity. A person who formulates an identity in existence by thinking that identity is separate from the basic Essence of Life is trying to plant their individual identity for their own benefit. But people who think of themselves as profoundly connected with the basic, immense essence of life will find a fulfillment that is otherwise not possible. When we are able to identify with the immense, formless essence of what divine presence brings to us, then we find the following list develop for us: "The fruit of the Spirit is agape, joy, peace, patience, kindness, goodness, faithfulness, gentleness, and self-control" (Gal. 5:16-23, CEB). Those spiritual fruits all go together. Of course, agape comes first because its spiritual power opens us up both to divine presence and to other people in such a way that what builds up for us is a profound sense of joy, peace, patience, kindness, faithfulness, gentleness, and self-control—in other words, a joyous well-being.

That deep spiritual sense allows us to accept other people in a life-affirming way that we become neither agitated with them nor attach any degree of importance to anything they may do to us. That's how we're able to live in a forgiving, merciful way. Even though we might think that is not humanly possible, with and through agape, all is possible.

When we look back to that section of 1 Corinthians 13, which contains negative language, we see that Paul was showing what happens when agape is not our motivating principle. He was describing the negative pattern of selfishness that messes up relationships and leads to so many problems in our world. He said that agape "isn't jealous, it doesn't brag, it isn't arrogant, it isn't rude, it doesn't seek its own advantage, it isn't irritable, it doesn't keep a record of complaints, it isn't happy with injustice, but it is happy with the truth" (1 Cor. 13:4b-6, CEB). Another way of looking at that list is to say that if agape is taken out of the picture, we're left with a very negative view of relationships.

Today, we look at that list and recognize descriptions of what gets built up when someone relies too heavily on the psychological defensive system that is called the ego-identity. Paul's list of negatives gives what, we would say in today's language, develops from trying to find our basic identity in existence from that little defensive ego we formulate from childhood's fears. So in our modern terms, we say that agape helps free us from being enslaved to that ego-identity, which is so dependent on thinking we are somehow separate from Creation. Instead, agape helps us be free to find our identity in connection with the eternal creative forces that are the basis of life.

Paul's conclusion seems to be based on a deep understanding of agape's origin. So his insight is that all the other spiritual gifts will eventually fail in their effectiveness, but agape will never fail (verse 8, CEB). And finally, even though we know that faith, hope, and agape abide to sustain us spiritually, "the greatest of these is agape" (verse 13). Greater than faith and hope!

All the meaning of those verses, taken together, shows me that the way the spiritual process works, people will not be forced to open up to agape, so each of us has to be not only completely willing to open our heart-center, but also that agape will eternally be there for us. Even though agape is the most important spiritual power for us, we have to freely accept the gift and use it, or else it will mean nothing to us. But without opening up to it and letting it work in our lives, we will not be able to find ultimate meaning.

That is why, after finishing those important verses (what we call chapter 13), Paul called his readers to "Pursue agape" (14:1, NRSV and CEB). Now, we can find many different translations of that phrase: "Follow the way of agape" (NIV), "Follow after agape" (KJV), "Put agape first" (NEB), "You must want agape more than anything else" (JB), "It is agape then that you should strive for" (TEV), and "Agape should be your guide" (CEV). It just figures that the Greek is difficult because what he is asking is not easy. We have to really work at it, spiritually, to aspire to have agape be our guide. It takes time—lots of time—and lots of trial and error. Of course, that's why patience is listed first in 1 Corinthians 13:4.

But no matter what it takes, Paul testifies that the effort is worth it. Because without that effort, nothing makes sense, ultimately. But it isn't only up to a man from two thousand years ago, it is up to each of us today. There is a fullness and a depth to living that is ready for us, and it also opens up a way for relationships to have more meaning for us. But what seems a little strange to me now is how much more my living and my openness to relationships have come to mean to me now that, finally, I recognize what Paul was

talking about. It helps to realize there is a word that could be applied
to that fullness and depth.

And when we look in Romans, we find an important statement
of his summing up of the basis of the confidence of his faith. He
talks about a special spiritual bond that agape can create:

> "Nothing therefore can come between us and the
> agape of Christ, even if we are troubled or worried,
> or being persecuted, or lacking food or clothes, or
> being threatened or even attacked . . . . For I am
> certain of this: neither death nor life, no angel, no
> prince, nothing that exists, nothing still to come,
> not any power, or height or depth, nor any created
> thing, can ever come between us and the agape of
> God made visible in Christ Jesus our Lord" (Rom.
> 8:35-39, JB).

The intervening centuries, after Paul recognized the basic reality
of that powerful bond, have brought a deepened understanding of
the promise of what agape holds for the spiritual development of
the human race. It is the power of agape that brings to the center of
our being the peace that is the profound basis of patience itself, the
spiritual strength of kindness, and the wise rejoicing in the truth.
Those people, who also realize the spiritual sensitivity deep within
themselves, have been given the awareness that they can be opened
up to ways to spread its influence.

Of course, we become involved in the spread of agape's
influence by letting it work in our relationships. That's what the
following chapters are all about. As the other steps of this method
of agape-praying came to me, I was inspired by continuing to study
those parts of the New Testament that contained the word "agape."

And so, to summarize, what Paul explained in his letters is
this: for those who open themselves to be receptive, they find agape
deep within as a gift from God; and then they can sense agape in

their relationships with other people, then to the rest of Creation in patient, kind, caring, compassionate, accepting, loving, respectful, and joy-filled ways.

Even though we know that agape does not originate from us, our faith development is strengthened by praying the process of agape working in the lives of other people. The more you work with agape, the more you experience the sensation like agape is flowing. We are strengthened spiritually by finding a sense that there is a connection between agape in us and agape in others. You may find an image coming to you of the flow of agape, first inside yourself, then between yourself and others.

CHAPTER TWO

To a Respected Person

*O*f the seven steps involved with the agape prayer practice, step 2 begins the process of holding other people in agape prayer. It starts with praying that the feeling you experienced personally in step 1 will happen in the life of a person you feel close to and respect. As you hold that person in prayer, you slowly begin focusing on imagining what that person's well-being would be.

For this step, you can choose a person who is especially important in your life, possibly someone who had an influence on your spiritual development (maybe even a mentor, teacher, or someone you learned with as you grew in faith). You should choose a person with whom you already have such a strong relationship that the person comes to mind when you think of God's agape working to help with personal well-being.

You may even choose someone with whom you feel a spiritual connection—an agape connection—whenever you deeply share with that person. You may bring to mind, in a time of prayer, a memory of an occasion when you sensed agape in an event or in a moment of significant conversation. That is one of the beautiful aspects to the spiritual power of agape that you can sense it working in your life as you share with other people and especially during a deeply moving worship service or a time of intense discussion about important personal or spiritual concerns. The more you work with agape, the more you experience the sensation like agape is flowing to and from the person you choose for this step, especially when you are studying with that person or with a group in which you are both involved.

But the first time you begin this phase of the agape prayer practice, you can honestly and truly pray for the well-being of the person you choose as the focus of this second step. In a time of prayer, you can visualize specific ways for well-being to develop in the life of that person. But you are not asking for something to happen; instead, you are holding that person in prayer. In a sense, you are spiritually sharing with that person, and this can happen whether you are geographically near that person or far away. Being in agape contact isn't effected in any way by distance or time. You don't even need to tell that person you are sharing in agape with them, but you will be amazed at the change that happens when you do tell that person.

There are different ways to be in agape contact. For example, in the time of prayer, you can imagine that person sitting next to you. Work with that image until you have a spiritual sensation of sharing in agape with that person. The sensation may even be of flowing, as though the power of agape flows from that person's heart-center or the center of that person's being.

But during all the steps outlined in this book, it's important to keep in mind that the prayer attitude for this practice is one in which you realize yourself as merely participating in something that is already happening. That's why you will experience a spiritual deepening over time as you continue this prayer practice. You will need to develop the sensation that this is what you are meant to do. In fact, "prayer" may not be an accurate word because we have to keep remembering that whatever is happening does not originate from us. It could even be called participating in a spiritual flowing from heart to heart and simultaneously to the heart of Creation. The spiritual experience is deepened by becoming aware (as we saw in chapter 1) that the basis for the divine power of human relations is not only already pouring into your heart, but it is also already pouring into the heart of the other person, and it is already flowing between the two of you. You only need to find the way to become aware of it.

So by prayerfully practicing holding this person with your attention as you visualize participating with her or him in the spiritual flowing of agape, you should experience the spiritual concern that this person will find personal well-being and deep sense of peace. That's why it might help if you form an image in your mind of what well-being would be for that person. If you know of a specific concern that person has, then you can be very specific with the imaging. You may even have a spiritual visualization with a double devotional meaning: of that person both being drawn close to divine Presence intimately and being opened to the vastness of Presence spreading throughout all Creation.

The first person I chose for this step was someone with whom I'd had many deeply meaningful conversations about the meaning of agape. We had explored the deeper understanding of agape during the years when I was coming to the awareness of the full implications of agape in human living. We had even spent time in a monthly prayer group, sharing deeply many of the tragedies and triumphs, heartbreaks and happiness, jam-ups and joys of life.

When I started this practice, I found that I was being opened up to an awareness of this person during a morning ritual. I have to admit that it took me several weeks to tell the person that I was doing this every morning. It was a new experience for me to talk with someone about praying for agape to flow into their life.

But the next time I saw this person, I was encouraged to learn that the person had started a similar morning ritual. That person had found special meaning by involving in the ritual the use of physical motion and a breathing exercise. That ritual was described to me as the following method. With an inhaling breath, the arms are crossed across the chest, then with the exhale, an agape prayer is sent to a person who is visualized. The inhaling is done while visualizing opening the heart to the flow of agape. As the exhale is done, the arms are opened with a gesture of the body, mind, and essence working together to send agape to a person held in prayer. Then at the end of the ritual, the arms are brought in across the chest to simulate a closing of the entrance to the heart-center. In explaining why breathing was part of the ritual, we shared our remembrance of the ancient Hebrew connection between breath and spirit.

When this person knew of someone who was especially respected and going through a rough time, that respected person became a special focus of this step of agape prayer. Later, I learned that on the evening of the first day of focusing step 2 on that person, the person phoned and said, "This morning at eight thirty-five, you came into my thoughts. My heart was suddenly filled with joy, and I felt blessed. What were you doing at that time?" The response was "I was breathing out an agape blessing to you." After a conversation about the meaning of agape prayer, the person responded, "No wonder I felt a blessing, and I thank you."

That is just one of many examples of the way the spread of agape has been going for me since I started this prayer practice. Small events happened for which there were no logical explanations. Connections were made in deep appreciation. Of course, it won't work that way for everyone, and that's the way it should be because those who try agape prayer will need to let it develop for them in their own way. We are merely participants in a spiritual phenomenon that has been going on for the centuries ever since it gained the name "agape." And yet, somehow, also for some people, it may feel like a brand-new development, like no one had thought about this, in just this way, ever before.

So not everyone needs to get that deeply involved with the first person for whom agape prayer is sent. A slow start may be needed for each person who tries this. And yet, because this comes across today as a new practice, it will take time for each person to let it develop. Don't become discouraged with the slow process. Take it at your own pace. It's important to let it develop in whatever way is best for you. And always remember to approach this with the spiritual attitude that you are not doing it; you are letting awareness develop of a spiritual process that is already happening. So even though it may feel like it is happening through you, it's important to keep the realization that you are not originating agape. You should keep in mind the attitude that agape is not originating with your everyday self but helping you gain the more profound awareness that you are merely following the divine presence manifesting the power of agape in the life of the person (or persons, in subsequent steps) you are holding in prayer. The people who do not block it will be amazed by what happens.

As you slowly, steadily increase the practice from step 2 through steps 3, 4, 5, 6, and 7, you may find yourself developing a deep spiritual sense of benevolence that seeks the well-being and happiness of others. And you may be surprised that it will not seem strange at all to find yourself seeming to feel like a pervading sense of compassion is welling up from somewhere deep within you.

Also, over several months of this practice, in which time is spent prayerfully following spiritual agape to bring well-being and deep joy to others, you will begin to experience a deepening of awareness of your own self-understanding, which at first may be a little hard to face, but eventually, you will find a spreading of peace throughout your life.

Obviously, this prayer practice should lead to action—from the power of agape actually flowing through your life's work, out to actively helping the lives of people and to the care for Creation. And that is another beautiful aspect of agape: it can be sensed flowing as you are actively involved in helping other people.

One of the powerful things about agape is that it works in our life in a learning way. So as we live, consciously, with the spiritual energy of agape, we learn to view life in a fresh, new way. Also, we find a fresh, new way developing, in a deeper sense, in our acceptance of and respect for other people and other beings in the environment. And we find out that such learning is not limited to intellectual understanding, but agape motivates us to put the deepening sense of acceptance of and respect for all into the work of caring and helping. At times, we are even led to working for justice and equal rights for people we might not have thought we would associate with before we started this agape contact. Agape truly is the *spirituality of action.*

CHAPTER THREE

To Friend and Family

S tep 3 expands the prayer practice to persons in each of two categories. The similarity of the two involves some type of nurturing. So this chapter is divided into two types of people: a friend and a family member. The order in which these are taken is not especially hard-and-fast; so for example, if a family member comes to mind first, then choose to focus on that person first.

The point for this step is to bring to mind a relationship in which there is a personal sensation of closeness, a feeling of being helped or supported and, in a sense, nurtured. Just as in step 2, hold the person in prayer. As you think about each of the two persons, a friend and a family member, concentrate on the feelings you have for them. As you hold each one in prayer, be very specific in visualizing that person. Then let your moment of prayer open to the flow of agape into that moment of prayer.

A Friend

Just to have a way to describe it, I'll start the description of this step with a friend. This choice should be someone who means a lot to you, possibly someone who gave you assistance in a difficult time. The person you choose can be a close friend who has sustained that friendship during many ups and downs in your relationship. You should choose a person for whom you deeply wish her or his well-being and happiness.

From an attitude of prayer, you should focus on experiencing the spiritual sensation of sharing in agape with that person. Picture the person sitting next to you as you pray together. Concentrate on your strong concern for that person. Find in your mind's eye what it would mean for personal well-being and deep sense of peace to come to the person. Work on sensing a deeper concern than emotions. In the time of prayer, find a spiritual sensation of what would be in that person's best well-being. Deeply sense that person experiencing the flowing power of agape in her or his heart-center. Think about what it means in personal detail for agape to work in that person's life to open their heart-sense to greater experience of happiness. Imagine that person being drawn close to and opening up both to the Presence in his or her life and to the vastness of eternity.

Practice holding that person in prayer as agape flows in that person's life until you can genuinely sense the soft, warm, comforting presence of agape for this person. Imagine what you think would make this person truly, profoundly happy, then hold that image in your heart as you pray for agape to spread in his or her life.

As you practice this for many days, try to find a deep sense of your relationship with this person strengthening and growing. If this person is geographically near enough that you can be with them, then let this prayer practice lead to action—to the power of agape actually flowing to this person when you are with them. Over the course of several months, you should do whatever is necessary to deepen your relationship.

But if you are not geographically near this person, don't let that be a problem because God's agape is not limited by space or time. The important point for you is to deeply accept that the person achieves personal well-being, no matter where this person is. This works because you are praying with the attitude of spiritually following agape as it flows in the person's life.

Some relationships that have developed over a long period of time go through different periods of emotional ups and downs and even have both agreements and disagreements, and there may even be times of difficulties or even hurt feelings, and so you may experience, during this practice, the surfacing of memories that carry with them confused feelings toward the person. If these feelings begin to interfere with your sensing the flow of agape, then you may want to stop the practice long enough to work through any sensation of blockage. In fact, if a memory surfaces of some act that requires forgiveness, then you may need to contact the person. But before actually making contact, be sure that you are able to look within yourself to willingly forgive whatever needs to be released. Only then, truthfully, are you ready to seek whatever reconciliation is required or directly offer the expressions of forgiveness that are needed. This is necessary because you need to be completely honest with yourself in order to be honest with someone else. You need to be completely honest with yourself in order to be able to be open to the Presence. You need to be honest with yourself in order to truthfully experience the flow of agape.

Paul touched on such problems when he wrote, "Agape must be sincere." He went on to give the following advice about the quality of living that comes from living by agape:

> Hate what is evil; cling to what is good. Be
> devoted to one another in brotherly love. Honor one
> another above yourselves. Never be lacking in zeal,

but keep your spiritual fervor, serving the Lord. Be
joyful in hope, patient in affliction, faithful in prayer.
Share with God's people who are in need. Practice
hospitality. Bless those who persecute you; bless and
do not curse. Rejoice with those who rejoice; mourn
with those who mourn. Live in harmony with one
another. Do not be proud, but be willing to associate
with people of low position. Do not be conceited. Do
not repay anyone evil for evil. Be careful to do what
is right in the eyes of everybody. If it is possible, as
far as it depends on you, live at peace with everyone.
Do not take revenge. (Rom. 12:9-19a, NIV)

There are several other translations of the Greek word that Paul
applied to agape in that first sentence: "Agape must be sincere."
It has been translated as "genuine," "non-hypocritical," "not a
pretense," "without pretending," and "without dissimulation." Of
course, these teachings from Paul will apply even more appropriately
when we get into the next two chapters.

What he seemed to have been talking about is our need for
the genuineness of personal relationship (or as Rollo May put it,
"authenticity in relationship" [*Love and Will*, 306]). Not only does
agape help with trying to work toward such a genuine, sincere
approach for relating to others, but it is a necessary part of the way
agape works. Paul recognized that need, and so he made the point
that through the spiritual origin of agape, we find the basis for
developing such authenticity.

Paul began that list of actions with agape because the list was
about the spiritual process that agape brings to people. The meaning
is the same as the list mentioned before in Galatians: "The fruit
of the Spirit is agape, joy, peace, patience, kindness, goodness,
faithfulness, gentleness, and self-control" (Gal. 5:22, CEB). We are
able to see that the list was all about what comes through agape
because that verse followed shortly after the reference to the second

great commandment (and we can gain deeper insight by leaving "agape" untranslated): "Serve one another in works of agape, since the whole of the Law is summarized in a single command: share in agape with your neighbor as yourself" (Gal. 5:13, the Jerusalem Bible [JB]).

And so again, agape leads us into the action of helping others. This understanding had an important historical origin, as we saw in chapter 1 when one of the great insights in the first century came as people seriously reflected about what Jesus meant when he emphasized a second great commandment and how the two great commandments were alike. This is what Paul was referring to in his summary of "the whole of the Law . . . in a single command." That was the way Paul expressed the link between those two great commandments as agape.

As I mentioned in the introduction, John expanded on the teachings about agape in the Last Supper section of chapters 13-15. There, Jesus instructs his disciples to share the power of agape with each other just as he had showed them what that spiritual power could do in human life and in relationships. To give the strongest meaning possible to this sharing, he told them that everyone would know they were his disciples because they lived by the power of agape (John 13:35). That is why he even put it in the form of a new commandment (John 13:34). He identified so strongly with the spiritual presence of agape that he could refer to it as "my agape"—as when he said, "Remain in my agape. If you keep my commandments, you will remain in my agape, just as I have kept my Father's commandments and remain in his agape . . . . No one has greater agape than to give up one's life for one's friends" (15:9-13).

You begin to live by that insight—of the link between agape for God and agape for a neighbor and agape for yourself—when you become aware of agape giving the energy to care for others and be genuinely concerned about other people's well-being as much as (if not more than) you are concerned about your own well-being. And if you find yourself in moments when you think that it is just not humanly possible to live that way, then those are the times to remember the true origin of agape. It is not generated by human efforts, but it is spiritual in origin, and so you need to open up to its power and let it work spiritually.

When Paul talked about being patient in affliction (Romans 12:12), that takes us back to what we found in 1 Corinthians 13:4 and 7 about what agape brings to living: "Agape is patient" and "Agape bears all things, believes all things, hopes all things, endures all things" (NRSV). We know too that patience is important in relationships, especially because of all the mistakes that are inevitably made in both sides of a relationship. That's also why Paul implies that agape is involved with the spiritual work of treating each other with respect. And of course, that's also why Jesus and Paul talk so much about forgiveness and not taking revenge.

Try to keep all that in mind as you practice praying for agape to flow for the person you chose for this step. It may take awhile for you to form an image of what you think would make this person truly, profoundly happy, but when that forms, hold that image in your heart as you pray to let the flow of agape go to him or her.

Another way of approaching this step's effect on you is found by thinking of a time when one of your friends was going through a painful situation. Your natural reaction is to want your friend to be rid of the pain. So you can approach this step by praying about a friend in pain. Let yourself feel the empathy of wanting the pain to end. Imagine what it would be like if you were enduring that same pain. Then pray, "May my friend be free from the pain and the cause of the pain." Then imagine the flow of agape helping your friend through the time of pain. Let an image form of your friend experiencing the joy of agape flowing throughout her or his being.

Then remember how that image felt for you when you go through the other steps as they are described in this book.

A Family Member

Now, we can think of our own family when we pray for agape to spread. The CEB translation of Romans 12:9-10 has Paul illustrating good relations by referring to the way relationships work in a well-functioning family: "Agape should be shown without pretending. Love each other like the members of your family. Be the best at showing honor to each other."

One of the multitude of joys I have as a grandparent is watching infants grow into toddlers. I watched my grandchildren develop and remembered how my children grew up years before. I have learned both how vulnerable humans are as they begin life and also how strong mothers are. When you watch an infant during the first several months of life, you see how very important nurturing is to humans. Each one of us begins as a very fragile creature, who could not survive without dedicated loving care. And the better the nurturing is during the first couple of years, the better the person becomes as an adult.

What that means is that we are born to be social beings. It is absolutely necessary that each human being has at least one person to care for him or her in order to survive for the first several months. We would die very quickly without that care. Of course, the larger the circle of help, the better the chances are for survival. But help there must be.

And when we watch a woman from the first few months of pregnancy through the birth and then the first year of her child's life, we are able to witness a sacrificial dedication that is truly amazing. Even though certain circumstances around a child may limit a child's nurturing to only one person, for those people who are raised by both a mother and father, the ability of two people to work together for the sake of the children is inspiring to the children. And like it or not, we have to admit that children are watching very closely everything that is done by the people close to them. Not much at all escapes the notice of small children as they grow.

But unfortunately, there are so many negative examples we hear about from around the world that we know how destructive it is when something interferes with the proper care and nurturing. When there is a lack of good nurturing during the first few years of life, then people have a very hard time as adults, and there is a lot to overcome. That negativity can actually multiply, and without a great deal of effort and self-insight, too easily it can happen that people who didn't have the good nurturing in their first few years of life will lack the basis to provide good nurturing, and that problem can get passed along from generation to generation throughout a whole society.

So the way human living is set up, we are meant to begin our learning in our family. It is in the family that we first learn about living with others. So it is the rough-and-tumble of family life that starts teaching each person often the hard lesson the hard way that other people have needs just like we have needs. In the give-and-take of the daily family activities, young children learn (or fail to learn) patience. But too often, that doesn't happen, and people grow up to be impatient adults, and then patience has to be learned in other ways.

I have a lot of memories of my family because my parents lived to be in their nineties. Their last several years were made very difficult because of rapidly deteriorating health. My younger sister was willing to move our parents near to her and her husband. And even though I lived hundreds of miles from them, when I visited, I watched a reversal in relationship roles that happens in a lot of families with very elderly parents. My sister became the caretaker of our parents. I have seen her and her husband provide much of the same kind of help for parents that they gave us when we were infants. This extends even to bathroom care. It was very gratifying to see how well my sister and her husband performed the reversal of roles and actually became the parents for our parents. So of course, I pray every morning for agape to flow for her and her husband.

In the closing years before my father died, I was able to work with the power of agape to change my way of relating to my father. Because he and I had problems in our relationship, for years, I had built up an attitude of not being willing to forgive him for the way he had treated my sister and me and also for some of the actions he had taken toward my children during some of the times when he had visited us when my children were young. Because of that inner struggle with the resentment I felt, I was very confused about the process of forgiveness in personality development. It took years for me to be able to understand the full meaning of forgiveness.

Only after I began letting agape work within me was I able to accept the awareness that forgiveness was something that I needed. Before that, I had blocked myself from seeing that forgiveness had to start deep within me. Finally, I was able to come to the freeing experience of getting out from under the emotional burden of resentfulness by forgiving my father. This only happened for me when I was able to realize that, first, I had to forgive myself for spending years of not being willing to forgive him. So finally, in the last years of his life, I experienced a true benefit from honestly praying every morning for agape to flow in the remaining period of life for my parents. I was able to find a definite strengthening of our relationships through the agape prayer.

After I shared an early rough draft of this book with my sister, she reported to me about her acceptance of agape and of her letting it flow in her relationship with our parents. It was deeply meaningful for her to realize how agape is always there waiting to help. When she was able to open to agape, she found the help she needed in bringing focus to her reaction to phone calls from the care center where she had placed our parents. Until then, she had felt like her nerves were jumpy whenever the phone rang. But when she opened up to the abundance of God's agape, she was able to find the calm and strength she needed. She found a renewed sustaining energy to assist our parents.

Finally, she was able to let agape guide her during the last two days of Dad's life. He fought dying with his whole body. Two days before he died, she could no longer watch his violent struggling, so she went home until she was called with the news that he had calmed down and had achieved a state of peace. She told me how much agape helped her during this time to bring her inner peace. That helped her find a sense of calm when the phone rang for the last time, reporting that he had died. I heard that calm in her voice when she called me with the news.

I flew there the next day. And so when my sister and I prepared and then shared with our mother a very personal memorial service for our father, we were able to remember and share memories of the times when our growing up was helped by actions of caring from our parents. Surfacing and sharing those memories was very important.

So as you search through your own family relationships, think back to your earliest memories or the stories you've heard or photographs of your family life. Realize what had to happen in order for you to survive. Bring to mind each of the people in the family or close to the family who helped you during your first few years. Then as you go through that list, let one particular person come to mind that you can choose for this part of step 3.

When an image of that person comes into focus for you, hold that person in prayer, then just as in step 2, let agape flow into that moment of prayer. Picture the person sitting next to you as you pray together. Concentrate on your deep feelings for that person. Find in your mind's eye what it would mean for personal well-being and deep sense of peace to come to the person. And again, it may take awhile for you to form an image of what you think would make this person truly, profoundly happy, but when that forms, hold that image in your heart as you pray for agape to flow for him or her. Try to keep all that in mind as you practice praying for agape to flow for the person you chose for this step.

Then work on sensing a deeper concern than emotions. In the time of prayer, find a spiritual sensation of what would be in that person's best well-being. Deeply sense the power of agape flowing for him or her. Imagine that person being drawn close to and opening up to both the Presence and vastness of eternity.

*   *   *

What we need to keep in mind as we go through the steps of this agape prayer practice is the divine purpose that makes agape prayer possible. Through giving agape to humans, God makes it possible for us to be able to find the spiritually profound level of intimate, intense affection such that we can give full acceptance and mutual respect to everyone around us. That insight will become important for the steps that follow. When we look around the world today, at the desperate need for people to learn to respect and accept one another despite the many differences, such as cultural, religious, ethnic/racial, and sexual orientation. We can gain hope from how agape helps bring humans to the existence that is divinely intended.

So in conclusion, we remember that when Paul talked about the spiritual meaning of agape, he said, "Don't hesitate to be enthusiastic—be on fire in the Spirit as you serve the Lord! Be happy in your hope, stand your ground when you're in trouble, and devote yourselves to prayer" (Rom. 12:11-12, CEB). He was showing the link between agape, happiness, hope, and prayer. That understanding is the basis of agape prayer practice.

Agape serves for us spiritually in a sense as a double way to open up our awareness. We can sense how it both works for us as the way through which divine presence manifests in our living and also empowers us to be agents for spiritual power to flow to our relationships and then spread to others. And so agape shows us how extremely important being in relationship is to our very existence. We are able to realize that we are participating in something so much more powerful than anything we could have developed by trying to identify in some way as some isolated, individualized personality.

Our awareness is opened up so that we can see the falseness of any attempt to build an identity that is based on separating ourselves from others and from the eternal formless Essence. That is how we come to realize that any identity we formed previously is nowhere nearly adequate. And so the steps in this agape prayer practice make us aware that we need a way to free ourselves from dependency on an ego-identity. Agape not only shows us that we have to start over with the formulating of an identity, but also agape helps us with that very difficult task. The sense of patience and kindness of agape helps with such difficult basic change.

As we move through practicing these steps, we also can begin sensing that the spiritual origin of agape means we are created in such a way that the basis of our being is accepting agape and sharing agape.

CHAPTER FOUR

To an Acquaintance

*N*ow we move to the fourth of the seven steps of the extended prayer practice. During this step, you will honestly and truly choose to hold in prayer a person who is merely an acquaintance or even a stranger who happens to catch your attention but who otherwise is not a friend. As you prepare to hold this person in prayer, hold yourself open to agape deep within, then let agape flow into that moment of prayer. You may pray the words "Let agape flow to . . ." as you bring that person into your mind's eye and be very specific in visualizing that person.

The point is to hold in prayer this stranger until you are able to let the flow of agape help you want the well-being of this stranger as equally strong as you did for the persons you chose for the previous steps. Of course, you will notice that, at first, you will not have the same attitude toward a stranger or a mere acquaintance that you have toward a friend or family member. So spend a few minutes thinking about why there is that difference in attitude. Eventually, you will need to come to the realization that for this prayer practice, your attitude toward the other person makes no difference. That's why it's important to constantly remember that agape does not originate from you. So you will need, during the time of prayer, to let agape help you get beyond your emotional attachments and attitudes toward the persons who are the focus of the prayer practice.

Visualize participating with this person in the spiritual flowing of agape. Pray until you are able to find the spiritual concern that this person will find personal well-being and a deep sense of peace. Work on sensing a deeper concern than emotions. In the time of prayer, find a spiritual sensation of what would be in that person's best well-being. Try to deeply sense the power of agape spreading from her or his heart-center throughout that person's whole being.

As you build up a true, deep concern for that person to find personal well-being and happiness, you are able to realize that what all people everywhere have in common is the desire to find personal well-being and happiness. This realization will become more and more meaningful, especially as you practice the next steps in this way of praying. You will begin to appreciate, in a deeper and deeper sense, the common humanity we all share, and you will find that such appreciation will steadily increase in meaning for you.

As you did in step 3, prayerfully hold this person with your attention. After you have experienced this process for several times, you will gain a sensation of spiritually sharing with that person, and this can happen whether you are geographically near that person or far away. Remember that being in agape contact isn't effected in any way by distance or time. Practice this exercise until you are able to visualize the person being profoundly inspired by agape opening that person's heart-sense. Imagine that person being drawn close to and opening up both to Presence intimately and also to the vastness of Presence spreading throughout all Creation.

Keep remembering that you are not originating what is happening. That's why your relationship with the other person makes no difference when you are working with agape. Your faith development is strengthened by becoming aware that the divine power underlying human relations has not only already poured into your heart, but it has already poured into the heart of the persons you hold in prayer, and it is already flowing between the two of you. So what is happening to you through this practice is a spiritual process of opening up to the awareness of that reality.

*   *   *

During the years that this agape prayer practice was developing for me, I continued to search out books that struck me as being somewhat similar to what I was experiencing. One such book has the title *Praying for Strangers.*[1] The author, River Jordan, described a prayer practice that had just enough in common with the step I'm explaining here that I was curious to read about her experiences. Her book is a shortened record of notes she took during a year of praying for a stranger each day. She began because of a New Year's resolution she made after her two sons were shipped out with the armed services, one to Iraq and one to Afghanistan. She knew she would have to do something extraordinary to keep herself from focusing too much on worrying about her sons. Each day, she would find that a stranger would catch her attention in a way that she would pray for that person at the end of the day.

After a few days of these prayers, she decided to work up the courage to approach the strangers and tell them she would be praying for them. When she finally was able to overcome her shyness and did that, she discovered that a level of meaning was added to the practice, and several of her strangers not only expressed a genuine gratitude for her prayer but some also even asked her to pray for something specific that they described for her.

Even though most of the people described in the book were people she met or saw in passing, one was just in a photograph of a newspaper story about terrible losses from a tornado. She was struck by the fear shown in the woman's face because it reminded her of how she felt when her sons left for their tour of duty. So that woman was the one she prayed for that day. But the photograph also brought back a memory from her childhood that made her realize that so many people share the common experience in life of suffering from tragedies. And she said, "We're all in this thing—the number and minutes of our days—together, and the sooner we realize that, the better for all of us." Her childhood memory that still haunted her was of the time her family's house had burned to the ground when she was only five. So when she focused her concern that day on the fear-ravaged woman in the photo, she found a little relief from her own fear over what might happen to her sons. She reported that praying for that woman stabilized her; it made her a better human being. And so she also whispered a thank-you to that woman.

She summarized the experience of praying for those people that year in this way: "They are rescuing me from a numb life, cut off from the rest of the world because I'm preoccupied with my own pressing needs. They are rescuing me from my indifference."

But what really struck me by the end of her book was her description of what prayer meant to her: "Perhaps one of the greatest human connectors in this world." She said that it was like "a 'chain' that runs from one carbon life-form to another, an unseen force that makes a strong vertical leap into the mysteries of the unknown."

As Ms. Jordan said about praying for others, "This one tiny thing that you can do can change the world you live in. It can change you." She reported that one of the changes that happened to her was learning to trust something greater than herself. I agree with her realization that this kind of praying for others does (sometimes very slowly) bring about a change in the person praying. There is an increase in trust—an increase in that quality of being human that is so vital to what sustains the very sustenance of relationships.

One of the things I appreciated about Ms. Jordan's book was her collection of quotes from other authors. My favorite was from Maya Angelou: "If you find it in your heart to care for somebody else, you will have succeeded." Another quote was from Mahatma Gandhi about the meaning of prayer: "Properly understood and applied, it is the most potent instrument of action."

But as much as I enjoyed reading *Praying for Strangers*, I couldn't help but think that she was taking a little too romantic a view of what a human being could generate by wishing. So there were a few times when she was putting a little too much emphasis on thinking, *This is my prayer*. She didn't seem to get beyond the attitude that she was generating the prayer.

So it's important to remember during the agape prayer practice that agape is not in any way being generated by you but is a flow that moves through you. The sense of prayer that you should develop is not one of directing but is more like you are merely following. In that sense, you could have that feeling that you are merely praying about where God already is manifesting agape. We remember how Paul did that in 1 Corinthians 13 when he talked about the spiritual power itself. He expressed the details showing what agape power could do. That was why he spoke directly about agape.

The Greek verb that is translated as "kind" is found only in that verse in all of the Greek New Testament, which means that it was an unusual word, so it must not have been what people normally mean as "kind." There was something else going on here. When Paul applied that unusual word to "agape," obviously he was meaning it in a spiritual way. Because in other places that strange Greek word carried the meaning of "wide-open acceptance," he seemed to be implying that agape was the means through which God makes our acceptance possible for us.

So what we have in that short verse (when Romans 5:5 is kept in mind, of course) is the great meaning that agape was implanted in each of our hearts for the purpose of making it possible for us to wake up to the trust that God is gently and persistently accepting us and helping us find spiritual power to help us in life. So one of the characteristics of agape as a spiritual power is that it draws us close to Presence in an intensely intimate way.

*   *   *

One of the points that River Jordan made in her book had to do with knowing the outcome of our praying. She pointed out that most of the time, with the people we hold in prayer, we are unaware of what is going on in their lives, especially in their minds but even in their circumstances. In that sense, we don't know the outcomes of our prayers. But every once in a while, we are able to hear from the person we hold in prayer, and we are told a little about an outcome. This happened to a friend of mine.

My friend had been concerned about what to do with an electric scooter called a Go-Go that had been left in her keeping after her sister died. My friend had already been turning to prayer to help her through her intense time of grieving, and she had sent out prayers for her sister, for all who love her, and for herself. Even though a long illness had made it obvious that her sister would not have long to live, when the end came, it was still a shock. She knew that many others were also praying because her sister had been such a big part of the lives of so many people. That led her to use prayer to learn what to do with the scooter that had become so important to her sister.

During the last several years of the very long illness, the electric scooter had been such a help for mobility and a sense of independence that it was important to find someone who needed such a help. For over a year after her sister died, prayers had not brought guidance for finding a good home for the helping device when on a warm summer day, an answer came to her in a parking lot. After an hour's drive to the nearest town, she arrived at the supermarket, where she and her sister had shopped, and she tried to find an empty space to park. The only one available was next to the handicap spot. As she maneuvered into it, a van pulled alongside into the handicap spot. That brought a strong memory of the many times when she had driven her sister in a similar van into that very place. After gathering empty shopping bags, her purse, and the grocery list, she opened her door at the same time the van's door started to open. She smiled to herself when the woman in the van said, "Oh, you go first. It takes me so long to get out." So many times she had heard her sister say those exact words.

After she got a shopping cart, she turned to see the driver of the van take a cart to the van so the passenger could use it as a walker. That brought another memory of the way they had used shopping carts the same way before getting the special scooter. The whole time she was shopping, she kept thinking about the similarities between the people from the van and her times in that store with her sister.

When she finished and loaded her bags into her car, she noticed that the driver had returned to the van. In a grace-filled moment of agape, she realized that her long months of praying about the scooter had been answered. She walked to the driver's window, introduced herself, and explained an offer: "I have an electric scooter that was very helpful to my sister before she died. Your friend might find it useful."

The driver was puzzled and replied, "I don't know. How much is it?"

"I just want to find it a good home. Now that my sister is gone, I want it to go where it can be used. So I want to give it to her." She described it and explained that it would need a new battery.

"Can we talk about it and get back to you?" They discussed details a little more, then exchanged telephone numbers.

By the time she drove for the hour back to her home and unloaded her groceries, she checked her answering machine to find that one of the messages was from the people in the van, who were accepting her offer. She called them and arranged a place about halfway between their homes to meet so she could give them the Go-Go. Their excitement over receiving the gift was contagious, and it became obvious that agape filled that moment of giving.

Several days after that she got a gracious thank-you note with examples of how much the gift was helping, such as allowing a family walk in the park to enjoy "the breeze and clean air, the trees and gardens," which were "all so wonderful." The note added, "Our hearts are full of joy and gratitude." But then came the explanation of a ripple effect on the handicapped woman's father, who "has been depressed and having a grumpy demeanor." For him, the gift from a stranger "changed his outlook and restored his faith in people."

*   *   *

It's good that patience is at the heart of agape because most of us usually make it harder for ourselves to let agape flow in our lives. That's also why nobody should get discouraged when there are a lot of missteps, start-overs, stops, and restarts that come with the agape prayer practice. That just seems to be the way it happens when trying to do this in our confusing, overly pressurized modern world.

Then, in a like way, each of the verses that follows from 1 Corinthians 13:4 should be understood in a deeper spiritual sense of how we can learn from the way agape works to bring about more meaningful relationships. When we concentrate on what is behind each of verses 5 and 6, we glimpse insight into the blockages that so many people let build up to bring problems in relationships. So first, agape overcomes any neediness that a person may let build up from the many fears we let grab ahold of us. It provides us with a sense of fulfillment that cuts through any tendency to desire to try puffing up our self-image by putting down someone else. Of course, Paul never heard of the concept of self-esteem, but when we read those verses after having heard about the modern emotional need to be strengthened in our sense of self-esteem, we can see how connecting with the power of agape can give us a basis more eternally sound than we could ever find by inventing ego-identities constructed from negative experiences we have in early childhood and the fears that keep plaguing us from infancy.

There is also an underlying meaning running through those verses that agape opens a person's heart-sense to supply the basis for working to achieve what is best for the human community. That sense of common humanity is meant in the original Greek of verse 5 (that is usually translated as "it is not self-seeking" [NIV]), but a note in the Anchor Yale Bible points out that it means "what does not belong to it"[2] so that when we translate it as applying to agape, we see it means that agape works against seeking selfish advantage over the common good.

And of course, once again, we recognize the need for action to come from this sense of common humanity, leading to working for ways to promote the common good in communities.

One of the many examples from the twentieth-century history was of a person who was inspired to help strangers because of a terrible rupture in the fabric of the human community. This was Raoul Wallenberg, a Swedish business leader. He has been called the person who rescued the largest number of people because near the end of World War II, he rescued about one hundred thousand Jews from being sent to extermination camps from Nazi-occupied Hungary. His story is often used to illustrate how much difference can be made through the courage of one individual.

When asked by the American War Refugee Board to be an official envoy from Sweden to Hungary, Raoul Wallenberg, age thirty-one, gave up his position as joint owner of an export-import company trading between Stockholm, Sweden, and central Europe, owned by Kálmán Lauer, a Hungarian Jew. By the time Wallenberg arrived at the Swedish Embassy in Budapest on July 9, 1944, all 437,000 Jews—men, women, and children—living outside Budapest had already been sent to be exterminated. The rest of Hungary's Jewish community was only 230,000 living in the capital.

Wallenberg's first job was redesigning the Swedish protective passport called the *Schutzpass*. His next step was crucial to ultimate success. In a section of Budapest designated by the Hungarian government as the International Ghetto, Wallenberg purchased more than thirty buildings as protected houses. There he set up hospitals, schools, soup kitchens, and a special shelter for eight thousand children whose parents had already been deported or killed. Because of Wallenberg's swift action in setting up shelters that offered care and protection, the other neutral legations and the International Red Cross also followed and helped greatly to expand the number of protected houses. After the war, it was established that about fifty thousand Jews living in the foreign houses of the International Ghetto had survived. Of these, about twenty-five thousand were directly under Wallenberg's protection.

On November 8, 1944, as the Russian army moved closer to Budapest, the Nazi official in charge of exterminating all the Jews in occupied Europe, Eichmann, ordered all Jewish women and children rounded up to be marched on foot for one week 125 miles in the freezing cold and snow, with no food or heavy clothing, to the Austrian-Hungarian border for deportation to the death camps. The men were brought to a work camp in another location. All along the route lay the dead and the dying. At first, the Hungarian authorities cooperated in rounding up Jews for the marches. As the first march started, Wallenberg went along the route of the march by car, giving out food, clothing, fresh water, and Swedish protective passports whenever possible. On the first day of the march, they rescued about one hundred people with the protective passports. A few others they rescued by sheer bluff. In the days that followed, Wallenberg made repeated trips along the march route and continued his rescue efforts at the border. He organized Red Cross truck convoys to deliver food and set up checkpoints for those with Schutzpasses. About one thousand five hundred people were thus rescued from transport to Auschwitz.

Eventually, Wallenberg was able to convince the Hungarian authorities to stop rounding up Jews for the marches. Then he redoubled his efforts to bring as many Jews as possible under the protective diplomatic umbrella of Sweden through handing out hundreds of Schutzpasses.

The Nazis called for the total massacre of the ghetto population. Wallenberg sent a representative to tell the general in charge that, if the planned massacres took place, Wallenberg would see to it that the general was held personally responsible and would be hanged as a war criminal. With the Russian army already approaching the city, the general reconsidered. He issued the order that no ghetto action was to take place. It was Wallenberg's last victory.

But the end of his story came with Wallenberg captured by the Russian secret police and taken to Moscow, where he disappeared in the prison system.[3]

Flowing through all the verses of 1 Corinthians 13 is the recognition that connecting with the agape, which is deep in the heart of our being, opens us to a stabilizing spiritual power that is profoundly calm and peaceful—so when it is working in our life, it brings about in us a calm, peaceful, restful effect. Paul was implying there that such is a kind of power that gives us the ability to emotionally step back to see the underlying truth of life, and that allows us to keep from being judgmental of others, and keep from having the need to take some perverted pleasure when others make mistakes or do wrong. Agape is the power to face reality in a deeply trusting and trustful way. By connecting with it, we are able let go of whatever from our past that keeps us from courageously working for the common good.

With that overwhelmingly positive appreciation of the power of agape, Paul is able to conclude that it is the basis of our faith and hope. Not only is it the basis, though, but of the three, agape is the greatest (1 Cor. 13:13). Of course, that gives agape the highest status, such that we should never try to trivialize it with translating nor diminish it with too simplistic an approach to interpretation.

Usually, the interpretation of 1 Corinthians 13:4-7 given by most people is that we are somehow to apply those verses to our personality. (How egotistical is that?) But usually, that's interpreted too simplistically and moralistically to mean something glib like the following: you should be patient and kind and don't be jealous or arrogant or rude or selfish or easily irritated or self-righteous; don't delight in evil but rejoice with the truth; and you need to put up with all things, believe all things, hope for all things, and endure all things. But like all simplistic moralisms, on one hand, those sound like a good method to live by, and yet on the other hand, it sounds impossible to live up to by applying only our very limited, human abilities. But when most people take that attitude toward those verses, the common response too often becomes something like, "Yeah, yeah, sure, sure." And then the verses are not looked into more deeply.

Too many people only want to learn on a superficial level. But the full impact only comes from learning in the deep, spiritual, transformative way. So as agape influences us to find a more profound understanding of life and then influences our way of relating to others on a deeper level, we are slowly transformed.

When we approach Paul's explanation of agape in 1 Corinthians 13, we need to use Thomas Merton's advice about the spiritual need to "go beyond the word and enter into communion with the reality." Only by experiencing the changes firsthand can anyone even begin to come to terms with the effectiveness of agape power to create patience and kindness and the capacity to endure whatever comes.

So this prayer practice is not meant to stay inside you. Instead, there is a motivational force to it. You should feel inspired to actually follow agape out into the relationships of your life—to feel the power of agape moving through your daily activity, out to actively helping lives.

Notes

1. River Jordan, *Praying for Strangers* (New York: Berkley Publishing Group).
2. Joseph A. Fitzmyer, 496.

3. Rachel Oestreicher Ternheim, *A Hero for Our Time* (New York: The Raoul Wallenberg Committee of the United States, 1981), www. raoulwallenberg.org.

CHAPTER FIVE

To an Enemy

S ome people think the fifth step is the most difficult
of the seven steps in this series of the agape prayer
practice, and so it requires a little different treatment.
This time, when you expand the prayer practice to include one
more person, choose to pray for a person who has done something
irritable to you or who might feel hostile toward you (even as
an enemy). At first, you may find this step to be such a strange
experience that it takes a lot more time to start this step than it did
to start the previous three steps.

As you face the difficult task of going into this step, it might
help to remember the old saying "Hate is easy, love takes courage."
We recognize that courage is needed because of the requirement that
Paul voiced when he said, "Let agape be genuine." When facing all
the feelings that come to us when we pray for agape in relation to
the person we choose for this step, we must find the courage to be
honest about those feelings.

(In case you are unable to bring someone to mind immediately as your choice for this step, try thinking through your acquaintances, and if someone comes to mind whom you hesitate about when considering that person's well-being, choose that person to pray for first.)

It might help to prepare for this step by remembering what you did when praying for the person in the third step; as you hold this person in prayer, be very specific in visualizing that person. Then let yourself open up to agape flowing into that moment of prayer. As the image of that person becomes clearer in your mind's eye, you may pray the words, "Let agape flow to . . ."

As you did in step 3, prayerfully hold this person with your attention, visualize participating with this person in the spiritual flowing of agape. Be careful about what would complicate this prayer, especially if you realize that negative feelings come to mind when you are focusing on this person because of past dealings with him or her. Of course, it's important to acknowledge that you still have such negative feelings (there's no point in denying your feelings), but don't let those feelings become a distraction. Remember that you need to find the courage to honestly deal with such feelings. It might help if you express those feelings to God in prayer, as did the ancient Hebrew psalmists in those strange psalms that gave voice to desires for vengeance (such as Psalms 139 and 140, where among other raw words are these: "Those who surround me lift up their heads; let the mischief of their lips overwhelm them! Let burning coals fall on them! Let them be flung into pits, no more to rise" [Ps. 140:9-10, NRSV]).

However, if it seems like those negative feelings are getting in the way, then you may have to stop this step for a while and go back to holding in prayer the person from step 4 as you shift your focus to someone for whom you have no feelings. Consider what it means for your well-being for you to have different feelings for the person from step 4 than you have for the person for step 5.

As you did in step 4, spend a few minutes thinking about why there is that difference in attitude between how you feel toward a friend, a family member, a stranger, and a hostile person. Of course, here we have to deal even more strongly with the realization that our attitude toward the other person makes no difference in this prayer practice. That's why it's important to constantly remember that agape does not originate from you. Also, pause to remember that God's gift of agape is already deep in the heart of the person you are holding in prayer.

Then when you sense that you are ready to go ahead and pray for the step-5 person in the same way you prayed for the step-4 person, pay careful attention to how you feel when you pray, "Let agape flow in the life of . . ." Visualize the person sitting next to you as you let agape draw the two of you into a relationship.

The point is to go through the prayer practice again and again until you are able to find the spiritual concern that this person will experience personal well-being and a deep sense of peace. After you have experienced this process for several times, you will gain a sensation of spiritually sharing with that person.

As you build up a sincere concern for that person to find personal well-being and happiness, you strengthen your understanding that what all people everywhere have in common is the desire to find personal well-being, deep satisfaction, and meaning in life. It is important to practice step 5 until you are able to honestly and truly think of this person as equally as you do about the people in the other steps.

As you develop the understanding of what people have in common and you think about all people having the basic yearning for well-being, deep satisfaction, and meaning in life, you will find a deepening of your appreciation of the common humanity we all share. The more you practice taking such appreciation into your time of prayer, the more you see the meaning to the need for people to find the way to treat people equally. Try to sense this as a spiritual need.

*   *   *

As I spent more and more time letting agape work in my life, the deeper became my awareness that agape was a common spiritual power in all people. This brought an awareness of an additional facet of meaning to the Romans 5:5 verse. I was profoundly impacted by the realization that the pouring of agape into the hearts of people was a basic part of the process of creation. So not only are we all created with agape in our heart-center, but as agape works in a person's life, it becomes possible to find that the deepening of relationships is a divinely inspired action. (Was that why John's section on the Last Supper showed Jesus giving his special teaching that agape was the basis of his new *commandment*?) So the power of agape has the full spiritual weight of being given to us by our creator. Therefore, the divine gift of agape has the purpose of helping people become divinely inspired to treat all people equally. So that's how it becomes possible for you to find the divine power of human relations pouring into your heart.

Even though the existence of spiritual agape in everyone's heart is the basic reality of human existence, it is not readily understood by a lot of people today. Unfortunately, in the modern world, a lot of people expend too much psychological energy trying to deny that basic reality of human existence.

A main outcome of these steps is for us to think of people equally and then let agape transform our approach to relationships that we are able to treat people equally. Isn't that what Jesus meant when he talked about God treating all people equally? ("For God makes the sun rise on both the evil and the good and sends rain on both the righteous and the unrighteous. If you show agape only for those who show agape to you, what reward do you have?" and "Treat people in the same way that you want them to treat you. If you share agape with those who share agape with you, why should you be commended?" [Matt. 5:45-48; Luke 6:35, CEB].)

In that way, you are able to see, eventually, that the categories used in steps 2-5 are arbitrary distinctions where agape is considered, and so you will come to see that dividing up relationships into such categories no longer makes sense. The process, throughout the steps of agape prayer, is meant to lead to a transformed perspective, such that all people are understood to share equally in God's agape.

Now, during the last several decades, more and more spiritual leaders have been calling for actions that I think of as an expansion of step 5. So even though it might seem fairly easy to practice this step with a person who has done something irritable to you personally, it might seem extremely difficult, if not impossible, if you were to extend this practice to enemies of your people or your nation. But that is where this step becomes important to apply to the problems of the modern age.

So this step can be expanded in a way that in a time of prayer, you can bring into your mind's eye someone the leadership of your nation considers to be an enemy. Find an example of such a person and hold this person with your attention as you pray the words "Let agape flow to . . ." then visualize participating with this person in the spiritual flowing of agape. Pray until you are able to find the spiritual concern that a declared enemy will find personal well-being and a deep sense of peace. Try to reconnect with that appreciation of the common humanity we all share.

It might help to remember the following collection of the teachings of Jesus: "But I say to you, share agape with your enemies and pray for those who harass you because of your faith so that you will be acting as children of your Father who is in heaven . . . . Therefore, just as your heavenly Father is complete in showing agape to everyone, so also you must be complete . . . . Blessed are the merciful, for they will receive mercy . . . . Blessed are the peacemakers, for they will be called the children of God . . . . Blessed are you when people revile you and persecute you and utter all kinds of evil against you falsely on my account . . . . You have heard that it was said, 'An eye for an eye and a tooth for a tooth,' but I say to you, Do not resist an evildoer; but if someone strikes you on the right cheek, turn the other also," and "I give you a new commandment: share agape with each other. Just as I have shared agape with you, so you also must share agape with each other. This is how everyone will know that you are my disciples" (Matt. 5:44-48, 7-39; John 13:34-35, CEB).

Or as we find in Luke, "But I say to you who are willing to hear: Agapao your enemies; do good to those who hate you. Bless those who curse you. Pray for those who mistreat you. If someone slaps you on the cheek, offer the other one as well. If someone takes your coat, don't withhold your shirt either. Give to everyone who asks and don't demand your things back from those that take them. Treat people in the same way that you want them to treat you. If you agapao those who agapao you, why should you be commended? . . . Agapao your enemies; do good and lend expecting nothing in return. If you do, you will have a great reward. You will be acting as children of the Most High act, for he is kind to ungrateful and wicked people. Be compassionate, just as your Father is compassionate. Don't judge, and you won't be judged. Don't condemn, and you won't be condemned. Forgive, and you will be forgiven" (Luke 6:27-37, CEB).

Paul expanded on that theme in Romans 12:14-21, a section in which he describes how people are influenced by agape: "Bless people who harass you—bless and don't curse them . . . . Consider everyone as equal, and don't think you're better than anyone else . . . . Don't try to take revenge for yourselves . . . . Instead, if your enemy is hungry, feed him; if he is thirsty, give him drink."

As I pointed out in my introduction, when Martin Luther King talked about those verses quoted above from Matthew and Luke, he pointed out that "agape" is what was meant there, not what modern Americans think of when they use the word "love."[1] So in the following quote from Rev. King, I'll follow through on that idea and change "love" to "agape": "Hatred paralyzes life; agape releases it. Hatred confuses life; agape harmonizes it. Hatred darkens life;

agape illumines it."[2] Another quote where I think the meaning is clearer when "love" is changed to "agape" is when he says this:

> Everybody can be great . . . . because anybody can serve. You don't have to have a college degree to serve. You don't have to make your subject and verb agree to serve. You only need a heart full of grace . . . . a soul generated by agape.[3]

So also, I would say that agape was what he was talking about when he described "the most durable power in the world" as "this creative force, so beautifully exemplified in the life of our Christ, is the most potent instrument available in mankind's quest for peace and security."[4] Of course, when we look back, we remember that at the time when he made such statements, he was directly witnessing the suffering brought to so many people by forms of hatred happening to innocent victims as well as to himself and all the other courageous workers in the Civil Rights Movement. And so I think he had the power of agape in mind when he said, "Do to us what you will, and we shall continue to love you. Bomb our homes and threaten our children, and we shall still love you. Send your hooded perpetrators of violence into our community at the midnight hour and beat us and leave us half dead, and we shall still love you. But be ye assured that we will wear you down by our capacity to suffer. One day we shall win freedom, but not only for ourselves. We shall so appeal to your heart and conscience that we shall win you in the process, and our victory will be a double victory."[5] Of course, he was talking about agape.

Rev. King gave this use of agape power the name soul force, and he said of it, "We shall meet your physical force with soul force." He held it to be the key to finding a longest-lasting solution to the problem plaguing the modern world. He came to that understanding because he saw the evidence of the changes that can happen when agape power is let loose in situations that seem impossible to change. The working of agape had taught him to come to such a complete reshaping of his attitude toward the oppressors that he could conclude, "We must not seek to defeat or humiliate the enemy but to win his friendship and understanding."[6] And of course, one of the abilities that Rev. King showed was his ability to take a very long view of history and human destiny, for example, when he prophesied, "The chain reaction of evil—hate begetting hate, wars producing more wars—must be broken, or we shall be plunged into the dark abyss of annihilation."[7]

And he showed how deeply he understood the spiritual basis of agape when he said about putting agape into action, "We are called to this difficult task in order to realize a unique relationship with God."

So just as Jesus took the effort to point out that God treats everyone equally (Matt. 5:45-48; Luke 6:35) and when we see the spiritual basis of the power of agape, we know that it comes from God to help with relationships. Rev. King knew that, and so he was able to say that working with the power of agape is a way "we know God and experience the beauty of God's holiness."[8]

The religious historian Karen Armstrong, in her chapter "Love Your Enemies," wrote about Martin Luther King. After extensive quotes, she concluded that even though he finally fell victim to the hatred that was unleashed against him, "his commitment to compassion changed the world and his memory remains a constant inspiration."[9]

When Ms. Armstrong was describing our modern international predicament, she said, "We have seen the danger of ruthless retaliation that drives people to despair, ignores their needs, and refuses to take their aspirations seriously. We have become aware that when people feel that they have nothing to lose, they resort to hopeless, self-destructive measures."[10] And so she agreed with Rev. King that putting into action the power of compassion and forgiveness "was an absolute necessity for our survival . . . the key to the solution of the problems of our world."[11]

But some people might have trouble with what I've described in step 5 because of the necessity of forgiveness. But this becomes possible when we let agape give us the perspective that forgiveness is meant to help us, to unburden a psychological weight that feels as though pressing on our heart. Isn't this what Jesus meant when he explained that we would need a depth of willingness to forgive such that someone could wrong you not just seven times but seventy-seven times—and yet forgiveness is still granted (Matt. 18:22)? When Jesus used such gross exaggeration, he seemed to be saying that forgiveness is not something that has to do with what others do to us, but instead, it has to do with what is inside each of us.

Martin Luther King not only talked a lot about the power of forgiveness, but he put it into practice. He said that whoever is "devoid of the power to forgive is devoid of the power to love."[12] But in no way was this approach some wishy-washy way of ignoring evil. He had seen too many examples of the terrible results of evil. He took evil acts into full account when he said that forgiveness means "that the evil act no longer remains as a barrier to the relationship."[13] He saw forgiveness as a catalyst for human relationships because it creates an important atmosphere that is "necessary for a fresh start and a new beginning."

But Rev. King understood that something more was needed in order for such a "catalyst" to work. That is why he carefully explained that he was not talking about love in the way people normally use the word. And of course, in order to get to that "something more," he had to turn to the Greek language. So as we saw previously, he made use of the Greek version of the teachings of Jesus to describe "agape" as "creative, redemptive goodwill for all." Rev. King said that we need to understand the spiritual basis of agape in order to see why "only by following this way and responding with this type of love" can the relationship with an enemy be creatively transformed.[14]

As we learned in step 3, through giving agape to humans, God makes it possible for us to be able to transform our understanding of relationships so that we can find the profound level of intimate, intense affection such that we can give full acceptance and mutual respect to anyone. And Paul knew a sad lesson too well from personal experience with people—that such a way of relating does not come from normal human living.

That's why we take spiritual development into consideration, as Paul did with the terminology of the gifts of the Spirit. When he used such terminology in *Galatians* to talk about the power of agape, Paul said that agape is the first fruit of the Spirit. ("The fruit of the Spirit is agape, joy, peace, patience, kindness, goodness, faithfulness, gentleness, and self-control" [Gal. 5:22-23]. "All the Law has been fulfilled in a single statement: 'Share agape with your neighbor as yourself'" [Gal. 5:14].) Those verses mean to me that agape's spiritual power opens us up and draws us close both to divine presence and to other people in such a way that what comes into our being is a profound sense of joyous well-being. That deep spiritual sense allows us to accept other people in a life-affirming way such that we become neither agitated with them nor attach any degree of importance to anything they may do to us. And when we hear such impossible-sounding teachings, then—especially then— we know that it is God's agape that works within us to transform us to fulfill such teachings.

Paul talked about such spiritual power transforming us through the renewal of our minds. That transformation brings us the ability to keep from being conformed to the selfish, egotistical, violent pattern of the human world. Paul spoke to this transformation when he said, "So then if anyone is in Christ, that person is part of the new creation. The old things have gone away, and look, new things have arrived!" (2 Cor. 5:17, CEB) and when he said, "Don't be conformed to the patterns of this world, but be transformed by the renewing of your minds so that you can figure out what God's will is—what is good and pleasing and mature" (Rom. 12:2, CEB). The sad state of affairs for thousands of years is shown in people in every civilization on the planet who are falsely indoctrinated to think there is nothing evil about taking revenge against enemies. But Jesus came to show us the power to change all that.

That's why, as the agape prayer practice develops for you, it helps if you constantly keep realizing that these steps are only possible because agape does not originate from you but is actually the way the divine presence is made manifest to all that God creates.

Obviously, this prayer practice should lead to action—to the power of agape actually flowing through your life's work, out to actively helping the lives of people.

As it says in the First Letter of John, "How does God's agape abide if anyone who has the world's goods and sees a brother or sister in need and yet refuses help? Little children, let us share agape, not in word or speech, but in truth and action . . . . No one has ever seen God; if we have agape for each other, God lives in us and God's agape is perfected in us" (1 John 3:17-18, 4:12, NRSV).

Of course, that's why Jesus used the parable of the good Samaritan to illustrate showing agape to a neighbor. So it was an illustration of agape power in action. He was showing that agape had to lead to actions of helping people, even if those people were being discriminated against by the society or were members of a group that was hated by a group or nation to which we belonged. That parable also was an illustration of acts of justice-making. To the people who first heard that parable, Samaritans were considered enemies. So his use of a Samaritan was meant to break down barriers of prejudice between groups of people, even groups who historically hated one another.

Such understanding about relationships between groups of people leads us into step 6.

Notes

1. King, 44.
2. Ibid., 140.
3. Ibid., 140.
4. Ibid., 49.
5. Ibid., 48-49.
6. Ibid., 43.
7. Ibid., 45.
8. Ibid., 47.
9. Armstrong, 183.
10. Ibid., 181.
11. Ibid., 182.
12. King, 42.
13. Ibid., 42.
14. Ibid., 44-46.

CHAPTER SIX

To a Group

S tep 6 begins the process of expanding awareness of the flow of agape. This can be thought of as a circle that begins to expand outward. So as the number of people you are holding in prayer grows larger, you can think of it as the circle of agape that continually expands. And because it is a spiritual circle, the only limit to the expansion that you will ever sense is the whole of Creation. (This will be explained further in step 7.)

So step 6 takes us beyond the individual approach of steps 1-5. While each of those first five steps had us focusing on one person at a time, step 6 is to expand the circle of agape out to more and more individuals and then to a **group** of people.

During each step, you probably thought of other persons you sensed would be good to pray for so you could be in agape contact with them. So you could start step 6 by going back over each of the steps (for example, think of other people who have been important in your spiritual development, then think of other friends and family, then think of other acquaintances or strangers, then think of people who you've been told are enemies) to find people you feel you would like to bring into a time of agape prayer. As you do this, you may find yourself thinking of groups of people. See if one group stands out in your mind as a group to start holding in prayer.

A good group to start with might be one that you feel especially close to in such a way that when you're with that group, you become aware of being drawn together and opened to one another spiritually in such a way that agape is flowing among at least a few of those in the group. So it becomes easy for you to pray for the well-being of both the individual members and the group as a whole. Pray for the spiritual power of agape to flow through the group in a way that increases the caring, compassion, and closeness among the members. During this prayer, begin imagining how the increase in agape becomes evident in the way the members relate to one another. It might help to visualize an actual instance that shows an agape connection.

For my personal agape practice, the first example of a group that came to me was a church because I used the agape prayer every morning with the Colorado churches that I pastored and the one I attended in retirement. Because I'm still in contact with these churches, and they are still in my prayers anyway, it was a natural progression for me, as the agape prayer practice developed, to let them be the first groups for me to think about for praying for agape to spread throughout their members and their ministry in their neighborhoods. So I pray for agape to flow in the church to strengthen the well-being and the sense of mission.

Paul wrote about praying for the churches and groups in those churches. For example, he said, "I'm thankful for all of you every time I pray, and it's always a prayer full of joy . . . . This is my prayer: that your agape might become even more and more rich with knowledge and all kinds of insight" (Phil. 1:4, 9, CEB) and "I remember you always in my prayers" (Rom. 1:9b-10, NRSV).

An example, from the church I attended in retirement, came from the support shown to a woman in her late sixties who became crippled by a quickly developing rare muscular condition. Within a few short years of contracting the condition, she went from a strong, active person to being confined to a wheelchair. She was a retired schoolteacher, and over those years of teaching, she showed a deep sense of caring for her students. She had a strong, active mind and had a wide range of interests and involvements. She was a caring, dedicated mother and wife who showed that same outgoing way of caring to everyone she met. People seemed to be drawn to her, and she willingly helped anyone who would seek her out to gain her advice for all kinds of problems. And so it was very difficult for all the people close to her to watch her body just seem to give out on her.

After she was confined to a wheelchair, her husband continued bringing her to worship almost every Sunday. Those times among the church community were especially meaningful. Before and after worship, members would come to her, one or two at a time, to share their support. And several of us did what we could to help out during the week. For more than thirty years, my wife and I had grown very close to her and her husband. So of course, during the last few years of her life, she was a main part of my daily agape prayer practice. Because I already had started holding that church in agape prayer, I became especially aware of agape being shared between her and the other parishioners who gathered around her wheelchair. She had been involved with churches from early childhood, and even though she claimed that her staunchly practical, somewhat skeptical attitude to life kept her focused more on the ethical, social justice aspect of religion and so not interested in spiritual matters, she showed a very natural way of letting agape flow through her actions.

The end of her life came quickly. She was in the hospital for tests when her lungs lost the ability to sustain a strong-enough airflow, so she was rushed into an intensive care unit, where she was attached to a ventilator. The message quickly went through the church, and many of the members made their way to the hospital, which was about forty miles from most of their homes. For three days, people gathered at her bedside throughout the day and early evening. Although she could no longer talk, she was able to communicate by blinking her eyelids. A system was worked out with her blinking to an alphabetical chart so she could spell out a message that could be written on a paper pad. It was difficult seeing a once-vibrant woman confined to living out her life attached to a ventilator, with IV bottles and tubes around her. I watched a few first-time visitors approach her with shocked expressions on seeing her like that.

One example of the way she showed that she was extremely touched by the love that was coming to her happened when she started to cry, and at first, we thought she was in pain, but she blinked the message: "I am crying because I am so very blessed." And whenever I visited her to find one or two visitors already in her room, I could feel the blessings. The intensive care room was small and dark. As I would stand among the visitors and family members squeezed into the room, I would silently acknowledge the flow of agape that seemed to intensify with each new visitor.

I was in her room with her husband during a visit from our pastor a couple of days before she died. We were the only visitors at that time. Her husband asked our pastor to help us share an agape prayer with her, and the pastor answered "Of course" as he put his hand on the husband's shoulder. Slowly we moved to stand beside the bed, with the two of them on one side and me on the other. We stood there for a moment, with the only sound being the rhythm of the ventilator. As the pastor offered a prayer for agape to flow among us, we touched her arms and shared in an intense moment of agape flow. Her eyes opened after the spoken words of agape were given, and her way of looking into my eyes was very inspiring. I knew deeply that she was letting a new door of spirituality open for her. I could see that her mind was very clear and she was entering a time of transition.

When medical staff determined that the only way she was staying alive was by the machine, her family was gathered around to make the decision to turn it off. This was explained to her, and she was able to muster just enough energy to sign off on the decision by blinking x when shown the place on the paper indicating that she wanted the ventilator turned off. She died a few minutes after the ventilator was removed. The next Sunday during worship, she and her family were held in prayer by the whole congregation.

My memory will hold that example for years because of the many ways agape was shared among a group of people to bring divine presence to intensify sharing, support, encouragement, and inspiration. I remember the times in the sanctuary when a couple of people would kneel beside her wheelchair, hold her hand, and speak their words of support and encouragement. Several church members told me how inspiring it was to see the way she kept going as long as it was possible, not letting her condition stop her until the very end. As difficult as those last few days in the hospital were, the sharing of agape among so many people gathering to her became spiritually uplifting. After her death, her husband talked with me, through his struggle with grieving, about how much he was strengthened by experiencing agape flowing among the people sharing with her. Agape helped him deal with the gaping hole he felt in his life.

There is a church story from Romania in the 1960s. It's about a Dutch Bible smuggler, Brother Andrew. After he got a load of Bibles across the Romanian border and past communist guards, he checked into a hotel and asked the hotel clerk where he might find a church. The clerk looked at him a little strangely and answered, "We don't have many of those, you know. Besides, you couldn't understand the language." "Didn't you know?" Andrew replied. "Christians speak a kind of universal language." "Oh, what's that?" asked the clerk. "It's called agape."

When Andrew finally met with two members of a church, they sat staring at one another across the room until Andrew spotted a Romanian Bible, then he reached into his pocket and pulled out a

Dutch Bible. He turned to 1 Corinthians 16:20 and held the Bible out, pointing to the name of the book. They quickly found the same chapter and verse in their Romanian Bibles and read, "All the brothers here send you greetings. Greet one another with a holy kiss." These men spent half an hour conversing and sharing—just through the words of the scripture. Andrew was deeply gratified to see how happy they were to be able to find spiritual fellowship across different cultures. Their sense of fellowship was able to transcend language differences by using the Bible. This experience of crossing cultural boundaries lasted for hours as they laughed until tears came to their eyes.

At the hotel, the clerk approached Andrew and remarked, "Say, I looked up 'agape' in the dictionary. There's no language by that name." Andrew replied, "I was speaking in it all afternoon."[1]

When I was in seminary, I served as the part-time youth director of a neighborhood church. As I got to know the members, I found out that most of them were very active in service projects throughout the community. I helped the church form a Social Action Committee to try coordinating all that work and promoting those service projects among other church members. But after almost no success for a few months, I realized that coordinating was not something that church did. Support and encouragement was what that church did. So I learned an important lesson that helped me for the rest of my career. People don't need to serve in the same way. It's completely natural for different people to serve in ways that are appropriate for each person.

Paul showed his understanding of that insight in many ways, but the most understandable passage is in 1 Corinthians 12, where he compared a church to a human body. Just as a body has to have different parts functioning in different ways, so in a church the total work is fulfilled with various members fulfilling a wide variety of functions. When I take that illustration into the work of the wide variety of social causes, I can see that every person doesn't need to get heavily involved in every cause.

That insight was very helpful during my time in seminary because those were the days when social action causes were spreading furiously. Those were the days of the height of the Civil Rights Movement, the Vietnam War protests, and the Women's Rights Movement. And of course, there were still the various antipoverty programs. It was also the beginning of the Environmental Movement and the Gay Rights Movement. Soon after I graduated and was ordained, one of my fellow students became the first person to be ordained as an openly gay person. At first, most of the seminary students tried to get heavily involved in all those causes, but soon our discussions showed that such efforts were just wearing us out and were leading to negative attitudes toward those students who weren't involved. Slowly we realized that each person could pick which cause fit with the talents that each had, and then we could all support and encourage one another in many different ways. We could help celebrate the small victories, and of course, when failures happened, we could commiserate with one another and encourage the efforts to keep on trying. There was no reason to feel guilty that we couldn't do everything.

*   *   *

Other possible choices of groups might be a school or family or study class or neighborhood or housing complex. Pray to experience how agape is manifested among them. When I say pray for the well-being of that group, I mean in the same way that you prayed for a person in steps 2-5. Prayerfully hold with your attention a group you choose and visualize participating with this group in the spiritual flowing of agape. Then let agape flow into that moment of prayer. As you hold the group in prayer, you may pray the words "Let agape flow among . . ." And remember, being in agape contact isn't affected in any way by distance or time. Practice this exercise until you are able to experience the power of agape flowing into the center of this group's life and work.

You might want to expand to other groups by using similar categories to the ones in those previous steps, for example, expand from the spiritually meaningful group to consider a group of friends, then expand to a group of strangers, and finally, expand to a group of people from a culture or nation considered to be enemies of your own culture or nation.

As the agape prayer practice develops for you, it helps to constantly keep realizing that these steps are only possible because agape does not originate from you but is actually the way the divine presence is made manifest to all that God creates. So you are merely following God's agape into the interactions of a group.

Notes

1. *Wit and Wisdom* (May 6, 1998), quoted in onlinechristianforums.com/storytellers-stories/22661-speaking-agape.

CHAPTER SEVEN

To the Rest of Creation

*T*he final step in this prayer practice is more in the form of a massive expansion. Such expansion can be thought of as letting your prayer attention become aware of the vastness of agape in such a way that you can visualize following the flow of spiritual agape out farther and farther. Of course, any going from group to group or any movement in a geographical sense is only human perspective because, spiritually, the flowing is actually not subject to the human understanding of time or distance categories.

Some people may find that a lot of meditating is needed before the realization fully develops that God's agape is not limited in any way to human beings. Even though we may first experience it as Paul did as having been poured into our heart by the Holy Spirit. And so we find it deep within ourselves. But of course, we must fully realize that God's agape cannot be limited by anything. We may experience it as an expansion that seems to flow from us, but that is only our human perspective. It is the way the divine presence is made manifest to all that God creates. In that spiritual sense, agape prayer gives humans a sensation of following God's agape as it spreads out to all of Creation.

So from our very limited human perspective, our spiritual development is enhanced by accepting a visualization of participation in agape expansion. We find ourselves enhanced by the realization, by a spiritual sensation, of vastness to agape. This enhancement begins with what I call step 7, which can be thought of as visualizing a series of expansions as the circle of agape is understood to expand out and out to ever larger groups. A possible aid to putting it into words might be to think of step 7 as involving six expansions: as you pray to follow the flow of God's agape, you can think of agape spreading

(1) to communities (beyond the expansion experienced in step 6), (2) to regions of a country, (3) to nations, (4) to continents, (5) to nonhuman creatures, and finally, (6) to all of Creation.

Obviously, that list is not meant to be in any order because God's agape goes where it will. And praying to follow it is a long, drawn-out development. But the prayer practice has a profound influence on a person's faith development. So now, merely as a way to talk about them, I'll go from one to six.

The six expansions can begin by praying for more of the groups listed in step 6, for example, by going from your neighborhood or housing complex out to other areas of your town or city or suburb. Also, you could go from one school out to whole school districts.

Another expansion of prayer concern could flow out to a whole state, then out to regions of a country. Further expansion would be to nations near yours. Imagine how a future could unfold in which the consciousness of agape could spread and aid in bringing about creative methods for promoting justice and better understanding between antagonistic cultural groups and eventually produce creative ways to solve problems in relations between nations. Many religious organizations use similar approaches in their development of practices involved with praying for peace and working for peace, both locally and throughout the world.

Then expand your prayer for agape to continents and then out to the whole world. Let your imagination open up to creative ways for spiritual development throughout humanity. Envision the possibility of a world in which people could come together to produce long-lasting, creative ways to deal with international problems so that nations would no longer need to resort to military conflict to try solving problems.

When the inspiration found in John 3:16 is studied backward and forward, the implication becomes the following: God's agape is for the world (in Greek, "cosmos"), and Christ was spreading the eternal life power of agape to all.

And finally, as we remember parts of the Bible where concern is given for nonhuman creatures, we realize that, eventually, we need to extend our agape prayer beyond human communities. One of the many examples in the Bible is the way Jesus referred to animals to illustrate a point, such as, "Foxes have dens and the birds in the sky have nests, but the Human One has no place to lay his head" (Luke 9:58, CEB). And an example of the concern of Jesus for the rest of Creation was when he said, "Look how the wild flowers grow; they do not work or make clothes for themselves. But I tell you that not even King Solomon with all his wealth had clothes as beautiful as one of these flowers" (Matt. 6:28b-29, TEV) and "What is God's kingdom like? To what can I compare it? It's like a mustard seed that someone took and planted in a garden. It grew and developed into a tree and the birds in the sky nested in its branches" (Luke 13:18-19, CEB).

So we need to realize that, in the spiritual sense, agape prayer gives the feeling of following God's agape as it spreads out to Creation itself. So the last part of step 7 is to follow God's agape to all of Creation. That's why it's been important throughout all these steps to keep in mind that we are not the originators but are sensing the flow of God's agape.

If it seems too grandiose an undertaking to think of the whole planet, you can begin this final expansion of step 7 by choosing a place where you already feel especially close to the wonder of Creation, then practice feeling the flow of agape throughout that place. It would be even more helpful to go to that place and pray there, and then, when you have spent awhile practicing following agape flowing around the place, you may pray to follow agape to larger and larger parts of Creation.

This understanding developed for me at a place in the park where I go every morning for my time of meditation. One October morning, as I concluded an especially intense agape prayer for a friend, a gust of wind rustled the leaves of the branch that was bent in front of me, and I opened my eyes to experience the sensation of agape flowing before me. Even though my eyes were open, I was still in the moment of prayer and still filled with the sensation of agape flowing within me. I was overcome with the awareness that the agape I felt within me was somehow making contact with agape in a bush in front of me. (I realize that is not a very good description, but the experience is indescribable.) I felt as though agape was flowing through my senses, going from me and also coming to me. The spiritual sensation was one of participation in agape-sharing with all that was around me. I was profoundly aware of agape connection with the bushes and trees and grass. What I experienced was everything being alive with agape. It was as though I were being welcomed into that little place in Creation. The experience that morning has informed my daily prayer there every morning since then. And what has developed is the understanding of how universal the flow of agape is.

At first reading, these six expansions of step 7 may sound like something that is completely different from steps 2-5, but actually, these expansions are what agape power is all about. During deep prayer, you let the wondrous realization come to you in all the awe-filled power that the spiritual energy of agape flows through you as it flows through all of Creation. Each of us is merely part of

Creation, but the important point is that you *are* part of Creation. Agape makes it impossible for you to deny that basic dependence of your being. Through participating in the work of agape, we become opened up and drawn into deep awareness of our connection with all of Creation.

For example, the friend I talked about in chapter 2 related to me that when practicing agape prayer, he had sensed the following connection between agape with people and with Creation. Early one morning, when he was staying in a mountainous area of Colorado, he practiced agape prayer outside. Sunlight streaming through a misty fog made the dew-covered meadow grass have an electric light-green sheen as a breeze swayed the grass in intriguing patterns. He climbed onto a boulder to sit for prayer. As he slowly released the thoughts of personal problems from the previous week, he was able to focus on the flow of agape spreading from his heart-center. What was brought to mind was a person whose partner was having trouble with their relationship. So in this moment of agape prayer, my friend put his hands over his heart, breathed in agape from his heart-center, then flung out both arms as he spoke their names and breathed out the sending of agape prayer for their relationship. He experienced a natural rhythm to this ritual as a warm energy flow moved through him as more couples came to mind for him to hold in agape prayer. After he had finished sensing the sending of agape, he became alerted to a cool breeze blowing across the meadow, and he opened his eyes to such a strong experience of oneness with all that was around him that he began feeling agape connection with the soft breeze and warming sunlight. He felt it to be very natural to be in agape prayer with the gently swaying grass as the dewdrops glinted with sunlight. In that moment, he felt overwhelmed with gratitude for being alive and aligned with all surrounding him. He sensed the flow of agape through Creation. As he brought his arms together to cross his chest in the gesture of concluding the time of agape prayer, he was filled with the sensation of being sustained through the flow of agape with the rest of Creation.

*   *   *

So the six expansions of step 7 are the way you let yourself slowly and steadily become aware of your participation with the eternal flow of agape. And this becomes a way to open up to your awareness of being Creation. The development of that awareness is the basis for understanding your essential identity as part of Creation. And the profound acceptance of such a basic identity helps in the process of letting go of other forms of identity that have been falsely crafted from a negative feeling of being somehow separate from the rest of Creation. This acceptance has become increasingly needed as the modern world has produced many forms of pressure on people to think of themselves from the perspective that sees humans being somehow separated from nature.

In the past, all attempts to think of humans as separate had led to a major problem for religions. Such a problem became embedded in the development of religion from its beginning. All throughout the multiple centuries since humanity's ancient development, there have been those people who get carried away with their perceived need to feel like life is manageable. Now it has become so much of a problem throughout the modern world's rapid pace of change that there are people today who fear their lives are getting out of control, so they have tried to find some way to get control. They fear that such need is so strong that they even want to imagine that God is manageable. This is behind the basic temptation to limit God. Through the spiritual power of agape, working within you, comes the understanding of how to turn away from that temptation to use religious rituals to get God to do your bidding.

Such temptation conflicts with our understanding of Presence when we start thinking that Presence isn't everywhere. That includes the mistaken thinking that the Presence isn't inside us. Some people even want to go to the other extreme to overcome that temptation by either thinking God is a being way off in a place called heaven or wanting to think that God just plain is not involved in their living. But if the belief is in Presence everywhere at all times, then God is involved with everything, whether we are able to open our awareness of that involvement or not.

And of course, many cultures today make it very difficult to pay attention to anything for very long. In America, the attention span of so many people has been getting shorter with each new generation for over a century. So just because we don't happen to be paying attention, that doesn't mean it's not happening.

But my experience with agape prayer has shown me that a way to begin paying attention is to open up to the flow of agape throughout life. The seven steps outlined in this book are a way to train ourselves to come alive to what the power of agape can do to draw us close to Presence. So the practices outlined here are meant to show a method for developing attentiveness in a creative way that can apply to daily life.

Conclusion

After completing these seven steps of this approach to prayer, I hope you have been able to realize a deepened understanding that there is a basic reality in the heart-center of all people. It is important that we are able to awaken a deep awareness of a common reality that we all share. But like all understandings that come to us in life, the expansion of this understanding will go on for years, possibly the rest of a lifetime. Each of us may have to go through the seven steps again and again to gain the deep realization of how connected all people are.

When the awareness of that basic reality has been awakened, the possibility has opened before us to begin to fully comprehend what all people have in common. And further, it is possible to gain the sense of how we are connected with all of Creation. In this book, I attempted to show how that deep and yet connecting reality was recognized around two thousand years ago and given the Greek name "agape."

One hope I have, for the agape prayer is to recognize what it means for more and more people to open up to the flow of agape among all people. But of course, each of us can only start inside.

In that sense, we are working from inside out. And that's why it's so important to start this meditation practice inside you but also to accept that such a step is only the first of many steps. So each day (and often, each minute of each hour of each day), we start over with step 1. When we do, we find that the spiritual action of going through the other steps will help with step 1 because all this is a process of opening up to the influence of Presence.

So from that perspective, the fruitful outcome of all these steps, even though they may not be fully realized for a whole lifetime, is cultivating within our consciousness a lasting commitment to deep caring. But recognizing such an outcome is not the important point because our growth along the path is more important, even though it may not be a straight or fast path, and we may not feel like we ever come to an end of the path. There may be times when we suddenly sense an amazing openness to agape, but there will be many times when we have a hard time staying aware of the flow of agape. But when we stop and look back over how these steps are working for us, such reflection can help us sense a development of deep caring.

The flow of agape nurtures that deep sense. We can think of the way flowing water aids in plant growth. That kind of nurturing in the growth process is what we saw as an illustration used by Jesus when he said, "What's a good image for God's kingdom? What parable can I use to explain it? Consider a mustard seed. When scattered on the ground, it's the smallest of all the seeds on the earth; but when it's planted, it grows and becomes the largest of all vegetable plants. It produces such large branches that the birds in the sky are able to nest in its shade" (Mark 4:30-32, CEB). So if this agape prayer practice seems like an awfully minuscule and weak approach when faced with the magnitude of problems threatening such destruction caused by people around our planet, then we need the encouraging awareness that size doesn't matter when talking about the way divine action manifests to us.

Another insight from that teaching of Jesus comes when we try answering the question, why was he asking people to look for an image for God's kingdom? Of course, when we, in America, look for an answer, we have to start by using a different term than "kingdom" because we no longer think in terms of imperial theology. American history has been able to demonstrate to other nations that the spiritual development of the human race was messed up during the thousands of years when the kingship model was used to order societies. So since we Americans finally have been able to demonstrate that people don't need kings, emperors, princes, and all forms of royalty, then it makes no sense for us to use "kingdom" as a theological model. And of course, for about fifty years, we've been slowly moving away from gender-specific language that would refer to God as king.

Such understanding makes answering the question easier for us today than at any time in the past because it seems that Jesus was trying to redefine what had become the standard image. Why else would he talk in such a strange way? Why else was he trying to get his audiences to change their understanding of what God was expecting of them? When we think about what most people at that time were longing to happen, we have to ask why Jesus was constantly using images that were just the opposite. The phrase "God's kingdom" was a dangerous lightning-rod phrase to people who were suffering under terrible oppression from a foreign empire whose soldiers on the streets were constant reminders that the freedom to live in their own land had been taken from them.

So what was Jesus trying to do by taking that dangerous messianic concept of "God's kingdom" and talk about it with such a strange, shocking image as a tiny mustard seed? The popular wish in his day was for God to send a messiah to come crashing into history, leading a host of fiery angels to quickly rally people to form a huge army to bring divine force to kick the Romans and Greeks out of the Holy Land and thus save the people from their oppressive enemies by establishing a kingdom so powerful that no foreign power could oppose it. But Jesus spoke to the crowds using images that denied such a popular image. He was just the opposite of what they were praying to God to send them.

So Jesus was showing how wrong that popular image was. In that sense, it was like he was saying, "God doesn't work that way and never will." That would have sounded like a very shocking way to talk. Would there have been a lot of people who considered that he was turning upside down all their hopes and dreams?

The words and actions of Jesus showed a completely different understanding. He wasn't willing to pander to the frantic religious zealots of his day. (And so for the following two thousand years, people should have followed his lead and dismissed similar zealous desires when they were piled onto Jesus's memory. But history records the sad evidence that persecutions, executions, crusades, ethnic clashes, and even wars were carried on by other kinds of zealots, who falsely claimed that Jesus held the old wish.)

Then we look to other images he used, such as a pearl, good fish, yeast in wheat flour, a treasure hidden in a field, forgiveness of debt, equal wages, chosen guests, wise bridesmaids, charitable sheep, and an entrepreneurial servant. Those were all images that would have shocked his audience because they were so unusual and pointed to a very different way of living. When a legal expert showed that he understood Jesus's description of the two great commandments, Jesus told him that he wasn't far from God's kingdom (Mark 12:28-34). Or when he replied to a challenge from some Pharisees, Jesus said, "The kingdom of God is within you" (Luke 17:21, NIV). Or because the "you" is plural, we can read, "Don't you see? God's kingdom is already among you" (CEB). In the beatitudes, Jesus said, "Blessed are the poor in spirit, for theirs is the kingdom of heaven . . . Blessed are those who are persecuted because of righteousness, for theirs is the kingdom of heaven" (Matt. 5:3, 10, NIV). Those were all put in the present tense, not about some future hope. That means that Jesus brought a spiritual understanding of the "kingdom of God." And such an understanding was an extremely far cry from anything that most of the people were expecting.

Martin Luther King expressed a similar spiritual understanding of that expression, for example, in the concluding sentence of his important book, *Strength to Love*, he said, "In a dark, confused world the Kingdom of God may yet reign in the hearts of men."[1] So a better translation would be found by using spiritual terms rather than political terms. That means it makes much better religious sense to speak of the influence of divine presence in people's lives and society. So even though the expression would be a little too bulky, still a much better translation than "the Kingdom of God" would be something like "the spiritual influence of divine presence in our lives and our society."

What do most people with a strong spiritual life say when they reflect back on the beginning of their faith journey? The usual response is a description that sounds a lot like a seed being planted. And the influence of God's presence in our lives is like something that grows strong through nurturing, coming from the depths of our being to profoundly influence our whole perspective on life. In that sense, agape fits into the description of planting and nurturing a mustard seed. And to stretch the metaphor a little further, we also recognize that plants grow slowly in irregular fits and starts and that there are even periods when it seems like they are dormant. Such metaphorical awareness can be comforting when we face irregular fits and starts in our spiritual development and even when we face dry spells when our spiritual development seems to be dormant.

The metaphor would apply to the way spiritual agape has been planted in our hearts to nurture our awakening as we slowly grow in our consciousness of spiritual power in our relationships. Such growth could then be called agape consciousness. That's how we become aware of the spiritual influence of Presence. So as we act on that influence in our relationships, feeling the power of patience and experiencing the growth and power of kindness (1 Cor. 13:4), we truly realize that there is a divine influence within us (or among us). That is what Jesus was describing. That is what Jesus was waking up in people's lives. And so that is what we need to open up to and allow to happen in our lives.

There also is a liberating aspect to agape's spiritual energy that lifts people out of enslavement by the pressures of the present, destructive era of history. I see such liberation as an important way of preparing for a new period of history that will bring a true, long-lasting basis for peace. The spiritual energy of agape has the power to liberate people from being conformed to the selfish, egotistical, violent pattern of the present era. Of course, the liberation of people's minds and hearts is not easy because the tremendous pressures from the human world are very difficult to overcome. The forces of this long era of history have been building up for the six thousand years of the process that has been named civilization. But if people resist agape's liberating power and are not willing to make the huge effort involved with living by agape, then their minds stay enslaved to the old pattern of the selfish, egotistical, violent era of history. Agape needs to be used as a dynamic and luminous influence against the power of the old historical pattern.

One aspect of the liberating power of agape comes to us to help us see beyond the accidental identity of our birth: everyone is born into a family, a race, a culture, a nation, but to form an identity based on such an accident of birth imposes limitations on the freedom of our being that end up holding back our spiritual development. One example of such limitation comes when people are forced to think they have enemies because of their birth. Of course, one of the strange aspects of the last two centuries is the way the enemies we are told to have in one period suddenly become allies in another period. When we carefully go through step 5 over and over again and then expand out to people we have been told are our enemies, we can begin to see how much our spiritual development has been held back by forces outside of us.

In her book, *Twelve Steps to a Compassionate Life*, Karen Armstrong explained part of her motivation for helping to found the Charter for Compassion with these words: "One of the chief tasks of our time must surely be to build a global community in which all peoples can live together in mutual respect; yet religion, which should be making a major contribution, is seen as part of the problem. All faiths insist that compassion is the test of true spirituality and that it brings us into relation with the transcendence we call God."[2]

And yet I've also noticed that a lack of emphasis on compassion allows the followers of religion to drift off into putting too much concern into areas that allow organized religious organizations to cause all kinds of problems. Karen Armstrong was concerned about how that drift allowed organized religious groups to let themselves be taken advantage of, and she said, "There has been much flagrant abuse of religion in recent years."[3] Unfortunately, such abuses have been going on for thousands of years.

Martin Luther King had the same concern about organized religion. He once said, "A religion that professes a concern for the souls of men and is not equally concerned about the slums that damn them, the economic conditions that strangle them, and the social conditions that cripple them, is a spiritually moribund religion."[4] As I pointed out in my introduction, when Rev. King talked about the Christian doctrine of love and when he referred to the loving purpose that guided him and when he referred to the way the power of love was shown in the use of nonviolent resistance to oppression, he was talking about agape. So we can see he was meaning the Christian doctrine of agape. We can see that especially in places like what he meant when he wrote from a Georgia jail about "an absolute necessity for spiritual maturity,"[5] he was meaning agape. And also, it was agape he was meaning when he talked about a liberating power, for example, in places like when he called that Christian doctrine of agape "one of the most potent weapons available to an oppressed people in their struggle for freedom."[6]

*   *   *

When we went through the Last Supper section of John, we saw that Jesus gathered his disciples to impress upon their understanding that they would be known by the way they shared agape with one another and then spread agape to others. So in the brief chapters of this book, I have tried to convey at least a glimpse of the vast implications of agape as the foundation of spiritual identity. Another way that Jesus approached that point about the importance of agape was to tell them to pay very close attention because he was giving them something new.

Also, we remember that the teaching was given the designation of a commandment. I remember when I first started deeply studying that new commandment, I was struck by a strange question: why did he call it a *new* commandment? I couldn't see an answer to that question until I left "agape" as untranslated. Now I see that the new teaching had to do with the power of agape. So during the last chance he had to give them teaching, Jesus wanted to make sure they understood the instructions about agape. And so Christians today miss an important point about who we are spiritually if we misunderstand the teaching about the spiritual power of agape.

As we become more accustomed to reading religious writings with an eye to what was probably meant when the word "love" is used in a broader or spiritual sense, we can substitute "agape." We can make other translations in the same way that we were able to take Rev. King's realization that "agape" was meant instead of the common English word "love."

For example, there is a famous internationally known prayer that has appeared in many languages beginning in 1912 and finally translated into English in 1929 in a *Quaker* magazine, where it was attributed to St. Francis of Assisi. However, in that prayer, because a spiritual meaning was being conveyed, we can now see that a better translation than the expression "sow love" is "sow agape." Therefore, I offer the following different translation:

> *Lord, make me an instrument of your peace.*
> *Where there is hatred, let me sow **agape**.*
> *Where there is injury, pardon.*

Where there is doubt, faith.
Where there is despair, hope.
Where there is darkness, light.
Where there is sadness, joy.
O Divine Master,
grant that I may not so much seek to be consoled, as
*   to console;*
to be understood, as to understand;
*to receive **agape**, as to spread **agape**.*
For it is in giving that we receive.
It is in pardoning that we are pardoned,
and it is in dying that we are born to Eternal Life.
Amen.

There also was a variation delivered by Mother Theresa of Calcutta when receiving the Nobel Peace Prize in Oslo in 1979 and when addressing the United Nations in 1985. Because of her work, I think I can keep the meaning by changing "love" to "agape" as follows:

Make us worthy Lord to serve others throughout the
    world,
who live and die in poverty and hunger.
Give them through our hands, this day, their daily
    bread
and by **agape** give peace and joy.
Lord, make me a channel of thy peace.
That where there is hatred, I may bring **agape**,
That where there is wrong, I may bring the spirit of
    forgiveness,
That where there is discord, I may bring harmony,
That where there is error, I may bring truth,
That where there is doubt, I may bring faith,
That where there is despair, I may bring hope,

That where there are shadows, I may bring light,
That where there is sadness, I may bring joy.
Lord, grant that I may seek rather to comfort than to
    be comforted,
To understand than to be understood,
To spread **agape** than to receive **agape**.
For it is by forgetting self that one finds.
It is by forgiving that one is forgiven,
It is by dying that one awakens to eternal life.
Amen.[7]

In this book, I explored the spiritual meaning of agape and so showed how much more it was than love, charity, and compassion. So when the common English word "love" is used to translate "agape," Paul's meaning was changed and made even more confusing. So not translating "agape" in English versions of the Bible was necessary to understand the religious consequences of what Paul meant when he concluded that of "faith, hope, and agape; the greatest of these is agape" (1 Cor. 13:13).

So as I conclude this book, I turn to the summing up that Paul did in Romans 12. Most of that chapter is a list of practical actions. He began by urging followers of Christ to let the Holy Spirit transform their minds so they do not conform to the patterns of their present age of history. "Don't be conformed to the patterns of this era, but be transformed by the renewing of your minds" (12:2). Agape guided by the Holy Spirit can overcome that most dangerous part of human societies—God's agape can actually break down that old worldly pattern of taking revenge against enemies that mistakenly tries to overcome evil with evil. Paul knew how truly that change was needed, partly because of what he saw going on in towns and cities from Jerusalem through Turkey and Greece, all the way to Rome.

Then beginning with verse 9 ("Agape should be shown without pretending"), he focused on the actions that spiritual agape helps us do when we honestly and sincerely let it open us to its spiritual flow in our life. He wrote about the way agape's power, when we let it work in our relationships, helps us work for good against evil. For example, "be welcoming and hospitable to strangers, and bless people who harass you" (12:14).

When describing good, healthful relationships, he gave the illustration of treating others as kind family members would treat one another—with respect, showing honor toward other people. Also, he showed how agape helps faithful people not be conceited or proud but live in harmony and peace with everyone, even to the point of blessing those you disagree with or who would persecute you. When he pointed out the strengthening aspects of agape, he described the way that spiritual energy helped with being patient in affliction (note, he didn't insinuate that we would, in any way, escape affliction—all the great lives from the New Testament, from Jesus to the disciples to Paul, had to go through afflictions).

When emphasizing the important power agape had with bringing empathy to people, Paul wrote, "Be happy with those who are happy, and cry with those who are crying. Consider everyone as equal, and don't think that you're better than anyone else . . . . If possible, to the best of your ability, live at peace with all people. Don't try to take revenge . . . . If your enemy is hungry, feed him; if he is thirsty, give him a drink. Do not be overcome by evil, but overcome evil with good" (Rom. 12:15-23, CEB).

And so finally, the basis of the spiritual meaning of agape comes down to the powerful conclusion in the First Letter of John. "No one has ever seen God. If we share agape with each other, God remains in us and God's agape is made perfect in us" (1 John 4:12, CEB). "Let's share agape with each other, because agape is from God, and everyone who shares agape is born from God, and knows God. The person who doesn't share agape does not know God, because **God is agape**" (1 John 4:7, CEB). "God is agape, and those who remain in agape remain in God and God remains in them" (1 John 4:16b, CEB).

What those profound scripture passages say to me is that from the human perspective, we are brought into divine presence through agape. That is how our awareness of Presence develops for human beings, and so from our perspective, God is agape. But because agape is not forced on us, we are left in the position of having to find it deep within ourselves. Unfortunately, that spiritual process of searching within is not obvious to many people. And so for them, the finding eludes them, and they feel they have no hope of knowing God.

And when we look back two thousand years, we see that it was because so many people had lost all hope of experiencing a connection with God that Paul wrote his great message of hope that God poured agape into our heart through the Holy Spirit. I see Paul's statement as a wake-up call. So Paul is proclaiming that the reality is already there, inside us, patiently waiting for each of us to find it.

When we become awake to the full meaning of that for our life, we realize that it is by means of giving us agape that we are given the possibility to experience being drawn into intimacy with Presence. In a similar way, as I look at the period of massive change of our age and as I see so many people struggling to find hope, I agree with Paul that there is hope in the spreading awareness of spiritual agape. That spread helps reduce the violence and destructiveness we hear about around the world. And so a new era of history is dawning.

Notes

1.   King, 173.
2.   Armstrong, 2-3.
3.   Ibid., 5.
4.   King, 168.
5.   Ibid., 32.
6.   Ibid., 169.
7.   "Prayer of Saint Francis," http://en.wikipedia.org/wiki/Prayer_of_ Saint_Francis.

Appendix

This appendix gives New Testament verses in which "agape" has been left untranslated.

"'You must agapao the Lord your God with your whole heart, with your whole being, and with your whole mind.' This is the first and greatest commandment. And the second is like it: 'You must agapao your neighbor as you agapao yourself.' All the Law and the Prophets depend on these two commands" (Matt. 22:37-40, based on a revision of the CEB).

(An alternate translation is as follows: *"'You shall share in the agape of the Lord your God wholeheartedly, and soulfully, and mindfully.' This is the first and greatest commandment. And a second is like it. 'You shall share God's agape with your neighbor as you yourself* [share in it*].' On these two commandments hang all the sacred way"* [based on a revision of the NRSV]).

"But I say to you, agapao your enemies and pray for those who harass you because of your faith so that you will be acting as children of your Father who is in heaven . . . . Therefore, just as your

91

heavenly Father is complete in showing agape to everyone, so also you must be complete" (Matt. 5:44-48, CEB).

"God agapan the world so much that God gave his only son, that everyone who has faith in him may not die but have eternal life" (John 3:16, NEB).
(An alternate translation is as follows: *"God cared so much to share agape with the world that God gave the only son, that everyone who shared in his faith may not die but have eternal Life."*)

"I give you a new commandment: Agapao each other. Just as I have agapan you, so you also must agapao each other. This is how everyone will know that you are my disciples, when you have agape for each other" (John 13:34-35, CEB).

"If you agapao me, you will keep my commandments. I will ask the Father, and he will send another Companion, who will be with you forever. This Companion is the Spirit of Truth, whom the world can't receive because it neither sees him nor recognizes him. You know him, because he lives with you and will be with you" (John 14:15-17, CEB).

"Whoever has my commandments and keeps them agapao me. Whoever agapao me will be agapan by my Father, and I will agapao them and reveal myself to them . . . . Whoever agapao me will keep my word. My Father will agapao them, and we will come to them and make our home with them" (John 14:21-23, CEB).
(An alternate translation: *"Whoever has my commandments and keeps them shares in my agape. Whoever shares my agape will share in my Father's agape, and I will share agape with them and reveal myself to them . . . . Whoever shares in my agape will keep my Logos. My Father will share agape with them, and we will come to them and make our home with them."*)

"As the Father agapan me, I too have agapan you. Remain in my agape. If you keep my commandments, you will remain in my agape, just as I kept my Father's commandments and remain in his agape. I have said these things to you so that my joy will be in you and your joy will be complete. This is my commandment: agapao each other just as I have agapan you. No one has greater agape than to give up one's life for one's friends . . . . I give you these commandments so that you can agapao each other" (John 15:9-17, CEB).

"Such a hope is no mockery, because God's agape has flooded our inmost heart through the Holy Spirit . . . given us" *(Rom. 5:5, NEB)*.

"The Spirit comes to help us in our weakness. For when we cannot choose words in order to pray properly, the Spirit expresses our plea in a way that could never be put into words, and God who knows everything in our hearts knows perfectly well what the Spirit means, and that the pleas of the saints expressed by the Spirit are according to the mind of God. We know that by turning everything to their good, God cooperates with all those who agapao God" (Rom. 8:26-28, the Jerusalem Bible [JB]).

"Nothing therefore can come between us and the agape of Christ, even if we are troubled or worried, or being persecuted, or lacking food or clothes, or being threatened or even attacked . . . . For I am certain of this: neither death nor life, no angel, no prince, nothing that exists, nothing still to come, not any power, or height or depth, nor any created thing, can ever come between us and the agape of God made visible in Christ Jesus our Lord" (Rom. 8:35-39, JB).

"Knowledge makes people arrogant, but agape builds people up. If anyone thinks they know something, they don't yet know as much as they should know. But if someone agapao God, then they are known by God" (1 Cor. 8:1-2, CEB).

"Now I shall show you a still more excellent way" (1 Corinthians 12:31, the Anchor Yale Bible).

"If I speak in tongues of human beings and of angels but I don't have agape, I'm a clanging gong or a clashing cymbal. If I have the gift of prophecy and I know all mysteries and everything else, and if I have such complete faith that I can move mountains, but I don't have agape, I'm nothing. If I give everything that I have and hand over my body to feel good about what I've done but I don't have agape, I receive no benefit whatsoever. Agape is patient, agape is kind, it isn't jealous, it doesn't brag, it isn't arrogant, it isn't rude, it doesn't seek its own advantage, it isn't irritable, it doesn't keep a record of complaints, it isn't happy with injustice, but is happy with the truth. Agape puts up with all things, trusts in all things, hopes for all things, endures all things. Agape never fails . . . . Now faith, hope, and agape remain—these three things—and the greatest of these is agape" (1 Cor. 13:1-13, CEB)

"Let all your things be done with agape" (1 Cor. 16:14, KJV).

"Agape must be sincere. Hate what is evil; cling to what is good. Be devoted to one another in brotherly love. Honor one another above yourselves. Never be lacking in zeal, but keep your spiritual fervor, serving the Lord. Be joyful in hope, patient in affliction, faithful in prayer. Share with God's people who are in need. Practice hospitality. Bless those who persecute you; bless and do not curse. Rejoice with those who rejoice; mourn with those who mourn. Live in harmony with one another. Do not be proud, but be willing to associate with people of low position. Do not be conceited. Do not repay anyone evil for evil. Be careful to do what is right in the eyes of everybody. If it is possible, as far as it depends on you, live at peace with everyone. Do not take revenge" (Rom. 12:9-19a, NIV).

"Serve one another in works of agape, since the whole of the Law is summarized in a single command: Agapao your neighbor as yourself" (Gal. 5:13, JB).

"The fruit of the Spirit is agape, joy, peace, patience, kindness, goodness, faithfulness, gentleness, and self-control" (Gal. 5:22-23, CEB).

"As a result of having strong roots in agape, I ask that you'll have the power to grasp agape's width and length, height and depth, together with all believers. I ask that you'll know the agape of Christ that is beyond knowledge so that you will be filled entirely with the fullness of God" (Eph. 3:17-19, CEB).

"Accept each other with agape, and make an effort to preserve the unity of the Spirit with the peace that ties you together" (Eph. 4:2-3, CEB).

"If we live by truth and in agape, we shall grow in all ways into Christ, who is the head by whom the whole body is fitted and joined together, every joint adding its own strength, for each separate part to work according to its function. So the body grows until it has built itself up, in agape" (Eph. 4:15-16, JB).

"Live your life with agape, following the example of Christ, who shared agape with us and gave himself for us" (Eph. 5:2, CEB).

"The grace of the Lord Jesus Christ, the agape of God, and the fellowship of the Holy Spirit be with you all" (2 Cor. 13:13, CEB).

"Take off the old nature with its practices and put on the new nature, which is renewed in knowledge by conforming to the image of the one who created it. In this image there is neither Greek nor Jew, circumcised nor uncircumcised, barbarian, Scythian, slave nor free, but Christ is all things and in all people. Therefore, as God's choice, holy and accepted in agape, put on compassion, kindness, humility, gentleness, and patience. Be tolerant with each other and, if someone has a complaint against anyone, forgive each other. As the Lord forgave you, so also forgive each other. And over all these things put on agape, which is the perfect bond of unity. The peace of Christ must control your hearts" (Col 3:9b-15a, CEB).

"The goal of instruction is agape from a pure heart, a good conscience, and a sincere faith" (1 Tim. 1:5).

"How does God's agape abide if anyone who has the world's goods and sees a brother or sister in need and yet refuses help? Little children, let us share agape, not in word or speech, but in truth and action" (1 John 3:17-18, NRSV).

"No one has ever seen God. If we agapao each other, God remains in us and God's agape is made perfect in us" (1 John 4:12, CEB).

"There is no fear in agape, but perfect agape drives out fear, because fear expects punishment. The person who is afraid has not been made perfect in agape. We agapao because God first agapan us. If anyone says, I agapao God, and hates a brother or sister, he is a liar, because the person who doesn't agapao a brother or sister who can be seen can't agapao God, who can't be seen. This commandment we have from him: Those who claim to agapao God ought to agapao their brother and sister also (1 John 4:18-21, CEB).

"Let's agapao each other, because agape is from God, and everyone who agapao is born from God, and knows God. The person who doesn't agapao does not know God, because God is agape" (1 John 4:7, CEB).

"God is agape, and those who remain in agape remain in God and God remains in them" (1 John 4:16b, CEB).

About the Author

Robert A. West is an ordained minister who has served churches in California, Pennsylvania, and Colorado. Within his churches he has been a counselor, spiritual advisor, teacher, and leader of youth and adults. Outside of his churches he has been a community activist, an advocate for the environment, education, homeless, refugees, human rights and peace. He has a master degree in the Philosophy of Religion. He is married with three grown sons and a growing number of grandchildren.